SWING BATTA!

SWING BATTA!

GARRET MATHEWS

Michigan State University Press
East Lansing

Copyright © 2001 by Garret Mathews

∞ The paper used in this publication meets the minimum requirements
of ANSI/NISO Z39.48–1992 (R 1997) (Permanence of Paper).

Michigan State University Press
East Lansing, Michigan 48823–5202

Printed and bound in the United States of America.

07 06 05 04 03 02 01   1 2 3 4 5 6 7 8 9 10

LIBRARY OF CONGRESS CATALOGING-IN-PUBLICATION DATA
Mathews, Garret.
Swing Batta! / Garret Mathews.
p. cm.
ISBN 0-87013-573-2 (alk. paper)
1. Little League baseball—United States.
2. Fathers and sons—United States. I. Title.
GV880.5 .M32 2001
796.357'62'0973—dc21
2001000316

Cover design by Ariana Grabec-Dingman
Book design by Sharp Des!gns, Lansing, MI

Visit Michigan State University Press on the World Wide Web at:
www.msupress.msu.edu

CONTENTS

Acknowledgments / *vii*
Author's Note / *ix*
Introduction / *xi*

Trying Them Out for Size / *1*
The Draft: Locking and Loading for the Season / *11*
Netting Some Backyard Kids / *25*
Learning To Play a Decent Game of Catch / *35*
Throwing Hotters and Visiting the Actors' Studio / *51*
Hitting Each Other Up / *59*
Opening Day—No Parade but Lots of Walking / *71*
A Life's Lesson from the Snottybutts / *81*
Wrestling Over a Tough Loss / *91*
Sliding Practice with a Lakeside View / *99*
Brinksmanship and the Kid from Right Field / *109*
Connecting with Your Son on Just Pennies a Day / *121*

Getting Hurt by a Fourth-Grader / *131*
Yep, It's a Visit from the Giant / *141*
Whoo, Whoo, a Big Run / *149*
The Road to the Tournament Doesn't Go Through Hawaii / *159*
The Pinch-Runner Steals the Show / *169*
And Grown People Wonder / *177*

ACKNOWLEDGMENTS

I'd like to thank my oldest son, Colin, who got me started in baseball back in 1988, and my youngest son, Evan, who kept it going. Thanks especially to Brett Belcher, Eric Jones, Sam Moore, and Alex Beck—the greatest of kids. Thanks also to all the parents, uncles, cousins, grandparents, and anyone else who rooted them on. To my wife, MaryAnne, for putting up with the backyard net and with kids running in and out of the house to use the bathroom. Also to all the dads I coached against. If you want your baseballs back, they're in the shed.

AUTHOR'S NOTE

Evan is Evan. The other boys are composites from players I've coached, or helped coach, over the numerous seasons. Much of what I wrote about either happened or would have happened if we had played long enough.

INTRODUCTION

This will sound crazy.

I'm a grown man. Mortgage. A job that I report to five days a week. A yard full of mole holes. A sump pump that needs fixing. All of which is supposed to make me, by definition, a certified grown-up.

So, come spring, what do I look forward to most of all when I wake up? The prospect of wheeling and dealing with other men and women this business day who are equally certified?

Nope.

The prospect that a miracle will happen and the afternoon will bring fame and fortune?

Nope.

The prospect that a miracle will happen and the moles will serve notice that this year's convention will be held down the road?

Nope.

Baseball practice.

Hitting plastic balls and tennis balls as we work up to the real thing. How to field bunts. When to tag up. How to duck and cover.

This is Minor League we're talking about. Ten-year-olds. Fourth grade. Kids who say "gaven" when they mean "given." Kids who say "pine cone" instead of "pine tar." Kids who are at least a decade away from declaring free agency.

But baseball is only part of it.

The real reason why I kick the covers off a lot higher this time of year is the opportunity to be with the boys. To be a part of their laughter. To say or do something they might remember after they've hit their final weak roller to second base. To teach them as much as I can about what I think is the greatest game ever invented because only children are eligible to play.

What about the spoiled big-leaguers? you ask. High salaries. Robber-baron agents. Per diems fit for a CEO.

Obviously, you haven't stood, as I have, behind the batting cage during hitting practice where the millionaires are free to be themselves.

Goosing each other. Busting chops. Pretending to be a belching locomotive as they run to first.

It's the unfettered joy of being on the biggest corner lot they could ever imagine with two dozen other guys in funny-looking pants as they take turns belting a bullet of a ball with a stick that just moments before was used to flip off an unsuspecting third baseman's cap.

Children, every one.

The only difference is that they have more of a reason to wear jockstraps and they know better than to ask their coach for do-overs.

Yeah, I'm the adult with the ball bag. The guy who'll make out the lineup card. The one who insists the boys not throw their helmets or argue with the umpire.

But I want them to know that not-so-deep-down this mortgage holder is really one of them.

During the course of the season I can be counted on to do the following:

- ✔ Bet that I can catch their best fastball bare-handed.
- ✔ Stage the muddiest of sliding practices in my front yard, further depreciating my property value.
- ✔ Ask one of the more unsuspecting players to go to the equipment bag and bring me a three and two pitch.
- ✔ Play countless rounds of "Glove, Glove, Who's Got the Glove?"

Any coach worth his sweatpants can hit fly balls to the outfield. I add a completely new dimension to the instruction.

"Take off your mitt," I say to the first participant, "and pick two teammates you trust the most."

The gloveless player is puzzled. Who would have thought baseball practice would include taking a leap of faith?

"Here's the game," I explain. "I will throw what I humbly call a Major League pop-up. At that moment, Trustworthy Player A passes the mitt to Trustworthy Player B, who promptly sends it to the gloveless player. He hurriedly puts the thing on while tracking the highly thrown ball. If he's quick enough, and if his colleagues don't mess up, the glove should be more or less in place when the ball comes down."

The players are hesitant at first, but soon invent their own catch-the-ball-under-great-duress challenges, each trying to top the other.

Such as: "Have fat Johnny sit on me and see if I can get up in time to catch it."

And: "That's nothing, Garret. (We're on a first-name basis.) Have fat Johnny *and* his big sister sit on me."

And: "I'll do a forward roll first."

And: "That's nothing. I'll do two pushups."

I'm open to all suggestions, and the glove-slinging continues until dark with results funnier than any sitcom on TV.

Then I take them to McDonald's and we play around some more.

Like I said, I'm not certified.

My youngest son, Evan, loves to go to events in which there's a built-in chance one or more guys will get hurt. Rodeos, kickboxing, demolition derbies—he could attend his first year of college on the money we've spent on tickets. And, hey, I'm a willing companion. Anybody who'd bruise his hand catching a fourth-grader's heater to collect a fifty-cent bet is going to applaud a well-executed haymaker.

Often as not I let boys on the team in on the mayhem. They pile in the car to laugh at the bull rider who hit the ground harder than Frank Thomas sliding into second.

I used to think I did this because I'm more comfortable with kids than adults. And that's certainly true, save for those rare grown-ups who believe a few rounds of glove-slinging make for the perfect close to the business day.

But then my other son turned seventeen, and I understood exactly why my car is filled with batting helmets, beefstick wrappers, and Pixy Stix residue. Colin's a great kid, even with that stupid soup-bowl haircut. But he knows what a lien is—the surest of signs that our roles have changed and we can never again be playmates.

Evan is ten, just one year removed from walking down the aisle in elementary school for the last time and officially becoming, by definition, no longer a little boy. That fifth-grade graduation ceremony will be mighty tough on his father.

It was bad enough the day Colin renounced his boyhood on

that same aisle. The next step was middle school, where there is hair under armpits, where there are girls he won't think are yucky, and where it's almost impossible to find a good game of "Pick Up and Smear."

A part of our firstborn was gone forever. Oh, he'd still show up for meals and he'd still want to come along if we went to neat places like the beach.

But he'd never again have the same innocence. Never again want to sit on my lap. Never again let me pinch his ears in public.

He was taking his first grown-up steps. Checking out the action away from the nest.

Which is what you're supposed to do when those first armpit hairs start coming in.

But that doesn't mean I have to like it.

I would keep them this wonderful age forever. Baseball cards, bubble baths, the poster of the baby wolf above the bed—I'd pull a giant freeze-frame.

But they get older. Every time. An inevitability I finally was able to accept with Colin, in large measure because I knew we still had Evan to be that little boy. The one son could take advanced calculus, respond to letters from college recruiters who refer to him as "Mr.," and stay out until 2:00 A.M. I learned to be glad his voice is deepening, and am often able to look at his baby pictures without misting up. Because I had the luxury of a younger model in reserve.

Now that one is positioning himself for that jaunt down the aisle, diploma and Discovery Zone goody bag in hand.

And there is no spare.

I think of our secondborn no longer having knobby knees. No longer wanting to wear a plastic fireman hat. No longer hoarding Skittles under his pillow. I think of the day that will soon come when he won't want to be with us except when I break out the long-distance travel brochures. And suddenly my afternoons with Evan—and his teammates—take on a new urgency.

It follows that, at home, I'm parenthood's biggest yes man.

"Hey, Dad, there are some kids in the backyard and nobody wants to go home. Can they spend the night and then the next morning go to the nice restaurant and when they ask who we are, we'll say 'Spits family, party of seven.'?"

"Yeah, but get one more to come along. Might as well set the world's indoor record."

A fitful evening? To be sure.

The noise. The toppled lamps. The dirty socks. The sleeping bags to trip over. The cola trail that's denser than some rain forests.

But one of these days my secondborn will be too old to think a mass sleepover is a cool thing. And the silence will be harder to take than any broken lamp.

Old age will come soon enough. No doubt I'll regret I didn't put aside more money. And I'll wish I had kept better track of the people who came in and out of my life. But there'll be nary a second thought about not being present and accounted for when my children were growing up, because I've had a front-row seat for the entire ride.

You can't defuse the ticking clock from adolescence to adulthood.

You can't change the setting.

You can't tell them to ignore the chapter on liens.

But you can tote the equipment bag, make out the lineup card, and holler for the demo-derby driver whose car's sum total of working parts would fit in his crash helmet.

You can understand it doesn't hurt all that much to fall over a sleeping bag. And that cola stains come right up.

Evan's not-that-far-away processional has convinced me that elementary school isn't nearly long enough.

It's a wide, wide world out there. Endless hours without recess. Sprinting down the hall to change classes. No Super Soakers to cool off with. Teachers who expect you to be at least somewhat mature.

Why rush into such a cruel, unfeeling existence? Why not have extended playing time on the monkey bars? More sliding practice. More glove-slinging.

The giant freeze-frame. Fourth grade forever.

Which is kind of why I'm writing this book.

To preserve the summer Evan was ten. And still a kid.

Like his dad.

1

TRYING THEM OUT FOR SIZE

A clipboard-carrying parent puts the ten-year-old boys in alphabetical order and tells them to stay in the dugout so they won't be hit by foul balls, and never mind if there isn't room for everybody, and don't play in the dirt because it just makes the dust worse.

"Sit on your hands," he suggests. "That'll keep them warm."

"I don't have hands, just batting gloves," one boy says. "Should I sit on them, or is that not the same thing?"

Ah, Danny. I'd know that squeaky, ever-inquiring voice anywhere. His parents are lawyers, and he's well on his way to joining them. I had him on my team last year and, when he wasn't doing the jitterbug in the batter's box, he was petitioning the court (me) for rulings on everything from who was better, Ruth or Cobb, to whether it was legally accurate to refer to the ball bag as a "ball bag" since it also contained catcher's equipment.

A stiff wind and two months' worth of sign-up sheets test the holding powers of the child-herder's clipboard. He decides in favor of a large rubber band and against taking Danny's query under advisement.

"Just sit on something, OK?"

Coaches group against the fence. Experienced mentors bring lawn chairs and sunglasses. Newbies get their pants dirty and squint. We talk about everything from the snow flurries in the weekend forecast to making fun of Technocoach, as we call him, who sends instructions to his team via e-mail. He won only two games last season, but he led the league in number of players attending computer camp.

Most of us know each other. If not, we bond quickly. We have the game in common, our sons in common, and we've all coached kids who write their names in the dugout dirt.

I see that Conehead, as we call him, is back again this year. You can always tell when his team is practicing because of the orange highway construction cones in the infield. Sometimes one of us will stop and ask if he's planning to build a road between shortstop and the pitcher's mound.

He just glares. You can kid him about being a trust officer and passing out visors with the bank's logo, but leave his cones alone. The guy uses them as targets for his catchers' throws to second. And to illustrate the limited distance a first baseman should stray from his position on a grounder to his side of the infield. And to show his third baseman where to play in a bunt situation.

At the end of practice, Conehead arranges his teaching aids at intervals in the infield and has his players run between them in serpentine fashion. The kids look like miniature conga dancers.

No better way, he insists, to increase flexibility and coordination.

Unless it would be road-building.

They nail me on two fronts.

The first has to do with my job. When are we going to get some decent coverage of our games? they want to know. The six o'clock news, ESPN, Bob Costas—you're our connection. Just arrange for a satellite truck to break down beside the field, they say, and we'll do the rest.

They're right. Give Technocoach five minutes with the instrument panel and they'll be watching our tournament in Istanbul.

But they save their serious skewering for my backyard batting net.

I got the thing for three hundred dollars from a guy who was going to turn it into fish traps if somebody didn't answer his classified ad by the end of the week.

The idea, other than to catch birds, is to have batting practice without having to beat down the weeds to find lost balls. The team gets more swing time, which is supposed to result in a higher winning percentage.

But that hasn't happened, and that's why my fellow coaches rag me.

To the tune of: "We hammered you big-time, and the only extended hitting practice we had was with Whiffle balls in a soybean field."

And: "What are you putting in this year? A foul pole?"

And: "If I ever come across any political prisoners, I know exactly where to take them."

At least the fish appreciate the net.

One coach starts to tell a "Joey" story from last season. A hush falls over the group. Joey is the stuff of legend. Big and strong, he can throw harder than many adults. He hits a line drive almost every time up. Defensively and running the bases, he has the savvy of a thirteen-year-old.

In coachspeak, Joey is the measuring stick for the other players.

Such as: "My Herbert hit a foul ball off him in the nine-year-old league and we celebrated with ice cream."

And: "My Sidney caught him in all-stars and broke his thumb."

And: "The ball was hit past shortstop into left field. I didn't think there was any way it would get caught, so I sent my runner. Joey takes off in a sprint from shortstop and makes the catch over his shoulder on the other side of our left fielder. In one motion, he whirls and throws it back in the infield for a double play. American Legion ball? Sure. But a third-grader?"

One coach says he's going to quit his job in ten years and become Joey's agent.

"Who said anything about waiting?" another coach chimes in. "I'll start next week."

The pitching machine is set on forty and every boy gets five swings. Then they catch grounders and pop-ups and make some throws across the infield. Coaches rate them in hitting, fielding, arm strength, and running on a scale from one to five. Scores are tabulated before the draft and the boys are placed in rows with others who turned in similar performances. You get one pick from each row and, yes, you must select your son.

At tryout time, the smart Minor League coach doesn't limit his viewfinder to performance on the field. For example, here are some players to avoid:

- ✗ Kids who wear shower thongs. Never mind how many balls they hit against the fence. I believe it's never too soon to make a statement on proper athletic footwear.
- ✗ Kids whose mothers have stuffed them into winter coats. I know from experience that these are the players who will expect me to turn off my car's air conditioner on ninety-five-degree days in June.

✘ Kids whose dads come to tryouts in "I'll-see-you-in-court" suits and carry briefcases that cost more than the bullpen.
✘ Kids whose dads spend way too much time in the on-deck circle helping them decide which bat to use.

Here are some players to take:

✔ Kids who have good-looking moms. Hey, it's a long season and there's usually at least one pool party.
✔ Kids who have sloppy, never-been-inside-a-courtroom dads who have baseballs, frayed jerseys, and unmatched socks strewn inside pickup trucks that haven't been cleaned in years. If they own a briefcase, it has a half-eaten ham sandwich in it.
✔ Kids who have dads who are powerlifters. Hey, the equipment bag can get heavy.
✔ Kids who wear tank tops to tryouts. A kid who isn't afraid of March isn't going to be afraid of the ball.

I pretty much stick to the point system and the occasional plus or minus by a player's name.

But some in the coaching cadre, most notably Technocoach, go beyond my primitive entries to include annotations on hustle, neatness, and even emotional well-being. I wouldn't be surprised if he requires his draft picks to have character references.

We're going to be married to these kids for three months, he says in response to being razzed unmercifully. You can't be too careful.

Conehead doesn't say much. He brought his orange pride-and-joys to the tryout and is miffed that the league director elected not to use them. Ballet rehearsals, he is told, are next week.

Even though all the boys are the same age, there's a wide talent gap.

Some can throw the ball barely forty-five feet, the length from the pitching rubber to home plate. Others can heave it on a line across the diamond from behind third base.

Some ten-year-olds wouldn't make good contact if the coach threw the ball underhanded. Others would get a decent swing if it came in at sixty miles per hour.

Some would rather climb trees. Others know how to compute earned run average.

The better players defiantly assume stances mere inches from the plate and actually look forward to the ball's arrival. The less skilled ones stand as far from the batter's box as possible, regarding it as a combat zone. Their feet are in constant movement, and some even put up a hand as a last line of defense against the ball.

In the field, the better players can range a few feet to their left and right to field a ground ball. The really chosen ones, the shortstops, can plant their back feet and throw across their bodies. The less skilled players don't approach the ball as much as tag along after it. After five or six bounces, even the most dangerous line drive has pretty much shot its wad.

Hey, it's not easy out there.

An outfielder endures interminable stretches of walks, errors, hit batsmen, and the catcher returning the ball a third of the way to the pitcher until suddenly, during Minute Number One Hundred of the game, a guided missile of a baseball is launched in his direction. The Cold War is over and he is unwilling to risk trying to catch the thing, no matter how easy his coach says it is.

Infielders are expected to dive Ozzie-like for grounders and then gun the runner out at first. This despite the fact that batted balls have been known to cause black eyes, cracked wristwatches, and shattered shower thongs.

All the kids like Pez candy, and bragging about being the first to buy the latest R. L. Stine book. They have green tongues from chewing watermelon bubblegum, and they sit in first chair at tonette concerts.

Sometimes we adults, in our hurry to promote them to the majors, forget this.

If you've never been to a Minor League tryout, here's what you've missed:

Chief child-herder, in loud voice: "Next, Bailey."

Bailey prepares to enter the batter's box, only to have his stance interrupted by . . .

Coach with sunglasses in lawn chair: "What happened to Asbury? It says on my sheet that Asbury is next."

Child-herder: "Asbury is at a piano recital. We told you that. You should have been paying attention."

Comfortable but confused coach: "Well, where's Arbuckle? Did you skip him, too?"

Child-herder: "Out of town at a chess tournament. We announced that when we ran down the list of gifted kids."

Coach: "Then who's the boy in the pink socks who just batted and got three hard hits?"

Child-herder: "Adams, and it was four hits."

Comfortable but frustrated coach: "Hey, no fair. You guys are working off a different sheet. No wonder I get bad teams."

Child-herder: "You've got the list from last year, shug. You need to shuffle your deck."

Embarrassed coach whose sunglasses can only begin to cover his red face: "Uh, er, my bad."

The good players ("fives" in coachspeak) stand at the front of the dugout and run their hands through the wire mesh. They're at ease with their bats, using them as swords or torches in a make-believe tribal ceremony. Hitting comes easy, a manifestation of aggressive personalities that drive them to cut to the front of the line at school and be among those who raise team trophies over their heads after the final out in the tournament. They can't wait to take the field because it's only a question of how well they'll do.

The not-so-good ones (in coachspeak, children whose parents have been generous contributors to the booster program) cluster nervously at the opposite end of the dugout. Their bats are tools that betray clumsiness and, thus, are not something to play around with. It's the same with their gloves. Leave them be until an adult with a heavy-duty clipboard and a penchant for ball diamond parliamentary procedure issues the call to that deadly reckoning ground that is home plate. They wait for first name, last name, and middle initial to be called—twice—before slowly walking away from the safe haven of the dugout. The only question is if they'll stink as bad as they did last year.

Veteran coaches, and I put myself in that number, don't pay much attention to performance. The most important thing is to be finished by lunch.

Evan goes in the hole to catch a grounder, lands more or less upright, and throws to first. He's not that good.

Joey socks one over the fence. He's that good.

Danny's best hit is a foul ball tipped against the screen in such a way that it locks in place, married to metal. He's not that bad.

It's March, for goodness' sake.

Bats spent the winter in the outbuilding next to the Weed-Eater; gloves are piled under the Rollerblades in the catch-all bin that's all but taken over the foyer.

The designated catcher of a kid misses the ball and the child-herder gets hit in the leg. Another kid overthrows first base, taking out two coaches. A kid whacks a kid while playing Robin Hood with his bat, and the angry mother is on her way to the field.

But how can we expect the boys to be ready when the adults running the tryout could find only two of the bases?

No Major League scout has to worry about me stealing his job. That's because my eyes are naturally drawn to the underdogs—hitters who step away from the ball, infielders who can't throw, outfielders who can't catch.

In our league, you're going to have at least three of these boys on your team and maybe more.

But it almost never fails. Over the course of a season, each kid will do at least one thing nobody thought he could. Get an extra-base hit. Tag a runner out at third. Score from second on an infield hit. Catch for an inning without hurting himself.

And he will do it because we've practiced. And practiced. And practiced some more.

I've discovered sharing this moment of success—and resulting joy—is the real reason I love doing this so much.

If spectators were writing a newspaper headline, it would read, "Miracle Happens: Tommy Covers Right Base on Bunt."

Or: "World Coming to End: Seth Sheds Thongs, Buys Cleats, Hits Ball to Outfield."

When these boys get older—and better—they're expected to field bunts properly. They're expected to have the proper footwear. They're expected to remember their gloves.

They'll deserve a coach who doesn't commit horseplay several times an hour. A coach more hard-boiled. A coach more certified. A coach who doesn't like it when a boy calls him by his first name.

Not me. I know my place.

And it's strictly Minor League.

The last ten-year-old runs to second base. I ask Technocoach how he graded the kid on footspeed.

"Gave him a four thirty-five," he says solemnly.

I look at his sheet. He's not kidding.

The pitching machine is put back in the shed. The two bases are collected and a watch put out for the third. A boil order is issued for the popcorn popper.

We coaches turn in our "twos," "threes," and "four thirty-fives" to the league director, who will crunch the numbers in time for our next get-together.

The player draft.

When we'll get what's coming to us.

THE DRAFT: LOCKING AND LOADING FOR THE SEASON

We file into the living room and receive copies of our evaluation forms as well as the row-by-row rankings of the boys who tried out.

I know about a quarter of the players personally and fifteen or so by reputation.

There are a half dozen or so boys to avoid because of poor attitudes. And a similar number of parents to stay away from because they get much too neck-veined during games.

You hear the whispers while the paperwork is being shuffled.

"That kid is a potential all-star, but last year he got so mad during a game he took out a pair of scissors and started cutting up his uniform."

And: "He's a great little boy, but his parents are going through a messy divorce and they scream at each other right on the field. I swear, the guy was getting ready to pick up third base and go after her. I was this close to calling the cops."

And: "He had a good first few weeks of the season, but then he started striking out all the time. I dropped him down in the lineup and when his parents found out, they said if they end up having to take their precious to a child psychologist, it's all my fault."

I listen to every word. And make mental "X" marks beside the players' names.

Don't get me wrong. I like to win as much as the next guy. I'm probably the most verbal coach in the league, constantly shouting instruction and encouragement. Every team has three or four good players, and I always hope our three or four good players are better than those on the other teams.

But the real world creeps in, even in Minor League. I would rather win half our games and have great kids and great parents than endure a season of bickering and infighting on the way to the championship.

Counting both sons, I've coached a dozen baseball teams since 1988. Only once was I glad when our team's time together was over.

Eleven out of twelve. Lasorda would have taken that percentage.

I scan the sheet and decide which players I want in each round should they be available when it's my turn.

Conehead draws the number one. This means he gets the initial pick of the first row, and then the last pick in the second round before returning to first again in round three.

It also means he gets Joey.

There goes first place, the rest of us whine almost in unison.

If you've never been to a Minor League draft, here's what you've missed:

Coach A, in been-there-before voice: "Whatever you guys do, don't take Steven. His mother can't stand it when he gets dirty. Once last year he didn't have a ride after practice, so I took him home. Little boy didn't want to get out of the car. Made me go around the block a few times like he wasn't sure where he lived. Then I found out why. I'm watching in the driveway while the mother runs out of the house screaming, strips him bare-assed, and takes the garden hose to him."

Coach B, in 0–10 voice: "Lord, could I please get at least one boy who can reach the counter at McDonald's without standing on his tiptoes?"

Coach C, muttering as he reviews the sign-up forms: "Why do I always get the boys from the swim team?"

Coach A, ever the historian: "Hey, if we get as much rain as we did last season, they'll be your best baserunners."

Coach D, by way of advice: "Don't take the Roth boy. He has absolutely no interest in playing, but his parents make him. Last year, he kept after me to tell his mother he had a good game. If I'd give him a good report, his mother would let him play after school with his friends. If I didn't, she'd make him stay in his room."

Coach A: "What did you do?"

Coach D: "Said he's a stud. I've got enough stress in my life."

Coach B, with one round left in the draft: "Can I go home now? I've already got all the bad players I need."

Coach C, with one round left in the draft: "I'll take Everett. His dad's great and his mother plays the harp. If the season goes down the drain, I can teach my kids a new musical instrument."

Graham's an easy choice as I had him the previous season. Excellent fielder. Hitting needs a little help. But, in my book, his scouting report goes far beyond how he catches the ball and runs the bases. Leads league in loving his dad. Not ashamed to hold hands with him in public. Brags that his dad played profession-ally for two years after college. Belches as much as the next ten-year-old boy, but always says "excuse me" even when he's miles away from being expected to have good manners. Sometimes gets words confused. Says "beam" for "bean," as in "I really beamed that guy today while I was pitching." In short, a wonderful child. Great company.

A few weeks after last year's season ended, Graham was walking home after school with two friends. Barely two hundred yards from the playground, a car jumped the curb and struck the boys. Graham escaped with a minor leg injury. One boy injured his hip. The other boy was killed almost instantly.

Dozens of parents placed memorial flowers on the sidewalk near where the boys were hit. We knew it could have been one of our own.

Later, I approached Graham's parents and asked if Graham wanted to write about what had happened. They said he had had some bad dreams and that revisiting that horrible afternoon might be helpful.

I turned his account into a column:

"We hadn't gotten very far after school when all of a sudden a blur came at us and I fell down. When I got up, I saw Bruce on the ground. I asked him if I should get help and he said yes. My foot hurt some, but I ran down the street (about a half mile) to my house.

"On the way I saw Luke's sister and her friends riding their bikes. I told them what happened and to go get help.

"A little while later, a neighbor brought me back to the scene of the accident. By that time, there were two ambulances there and a lot of police cars.

"I saw a lot of my friends standing around. The cops wouldn't let me inside the yellow caution tape until I told them I was in the accident.

"I was interviewed by detectives and put in an ambulance with Bruce. I pretty much knew Luke was going to die. It was a feeling I got when I looked around and didn't see him.

"In the hospital, they kept asking the same questions over and over. Then they told me Luke was gone. I knew he was in a better place looking down at me.

"Luke was a good friend. Every time I turned around he seemed to be there. He was kind of hyper and always had a smile on his face.

"We had a lot of things in common. We both played the piano and loved almost every sport. We would go to the field and play baseball. Luke was small, but he was a good pitcher because he had a good arm. We both liked the Atlanta Braves and we traded baseball cards.

"I don't know what Luke would have been when he grew up, but it probably would have had something to do with the weather. He was always looking at the reports and telling us if it was going to rain.

"I wasn't hurt too bad, just some torn tissue in my ankle. I left the hospital and went back home. All I felt like doing the rest of that Tuesday and the next day was sleeping. I was worn out from everything that happened. I felt guilty about being all right when Luke wasn't.

"I went back to school on Thursday. Every time I walked into one of my classes, the teacher would either smile or start crying. I ended up getting a lot of cards, flowers, and balloons from people I don't even know.

"His funeral was Friday. It was the first one I had ever gone to. His friends all wore black Nike caps in his memory.

"I miss Luke's smile and his good attitude about everything. I also miss how he loved sports just like me. Every time I see his parents or his sister, it reminds me of him.

"When I ride my bike past the baseball field and see kids playing, it reminds me of him and how we did stuff like that.

"It seems that people are driving a little safer in the area where the accident happened. I also found out that a lot of people care about others.

"I hope no other kids will get hurt the way me and my friends did. Life has more meaning to me now that I realize you can lose it at any time."

Graham wanted to know what I thought about his writing. A home run, I told him. Game-winner.

Caleb is a tougher call. An all-star, but has a screamer for a dad. Once got mad during a practice because he didn't think the coach was coaching hard enough. Grabbed a bat and hollered at the boys to report immediately to the outfield to catch fly balls. The result was an embarrassing clash of wills on the pitcher's mound. That was three seasons ago, but a bad scouting report on a father knows no statute of limitations.

But Conehead says not to worry, that the guy moved to Florida last year with his girlfriend. "Messy situation. Big-time child support. Came through our bank. Take it from me, he's too broke to visit more than once a season."

Conehead has been known to lie at these gatherings if it gives him an edge on a player—either to land an ace pitcher who's new to the league or to dump what he knows is three months of trouble onto another coach. But I trust him in this instance. Experience has taught me that when legal tender is involved, it's like giving the man a shot of truth serum.

I take Caleb. Maybe we'll get a rainout when his dad drives up.

Felix is a former player from three years ago. Another easy choice. He wasn't the greatest at catching the ball or at figuring out where to throw it when he did. But he improved over the season and became a better-than-average hitter. And he had a great dad.

After our first practice, Chuck told me how much he loves baseball and how he counted the days until his Felix would be old enough to put on a glove. His idea this season, Chuck said, was to volunteer to be assistant coach. Pick up the bats, help the catcher put on the gear, keep the kids quiet in the dugout—anything the honcho needed.

I told him I could use all the help I could get.

Chuck's face dropped. "But I can't. It's the stupid cancer," he said. "Some days I'm not even strong enough to get out of bed. No way you could count on me," he said.

It was obvious father and son had a special relationship. Patiently, Chuck helped me explain to Felix that the wise baserunner stays close to second on the extremely off chance—in the seven-year-old league—that the shortstop will hang onto the pop fly. He only breaks for third, Chuck pointed out, after the ball has been missed and subsequently kicked into left field.

I remember an excited Felix running up to his father and exclaiming that a teammate had thrown him the ball and he had actually caught it.

Felix scored the winning run in one of our games. A proud Chuck led the cheers. Arm in arm, father and son walked to the concession stand. Somebody should have taken a picture.

After the tournament, Chuck pulled me aside.

"I feel like I've let you down," he said. "This was my year to be with my son and I blew it."

"Next season," he promised, "I'll make it up to you. First-base coach, third-base coach, team mom—whatever you need."

"I'll look forward to it," I told him. "Just get well."

That was the last time I saw him. Chuck died five months later.

I select Adam, a kid I don't know and a kid who apparently didn't start playing until last year. Technocoach says he wishes he could have taken him. I don't know if this is because Adam has skills or is quick to answer his e-mail.

And K. B. Little previous history here, too. Came to the house last year to watch a baseball bloopers tape that shows players injuring themselves going after the ball. Naturally, it's Evan's favorite, particularly the footage of the minor leaguer who runs completely through the center field fence trying to catch a home run ball. Splinters for life, but a small price to pay for baseball immortality.

Danny is undoubtedly the best known of the kids who aren't all that good. The draft would have to wait while we exchanged stories.

There was the time he was told he was too short to play first base. Danny, all of eight years old and all of four feet tall, claimed discrimination.

There was the time he got a new glove, but couldn't get it broken in to his satisfaction. He bugged his father all evening until finally, after midnight, the guy agreed to run over the thing with his car. Having a properly broken-in glove, Danny told me, "will raise my self-concept."

Last year, I took Danny and some other boys on the team to St. Louis for a Cardinals' game. We came early for batting practice and the chance to get a ball. The other kids chased down home runs and pocketed the prize. All but Danny. When he was behind the left field fence, all the balls went to right. When he ran to that side of the field, the power display was to center.

His parents can afford to buy every item in the souvenir shop as well as probably half the players. That didn't matter. Danny had to have a ball from the field. He leaned over the dugout and asked the batboys for one. Nope. Then he offered five dollars.

Still no. Undeterred, he approached two pitchers running on the warning track. Nope. And no again to the five bucks.

Move ahead to the break in action prior to the home half of the fifth inning. The third-base umpire recognized someone sitting beside us and meandered over to exchange a few words. Danny, who was beyond frustrated at this point, asked him for a ball. Loudly. Scores of people looked our way. Little faces and one bigger one turned bright red. It was like farting in church. The umpire grinned and emptied his pockets to show the brazen kid he was fresh out of baseballs. Danny finally agreed to buy one from a vendor. I convinced him it would help the guy's self-concept.

I pick him again this year. Hey, I need an intellectual equal.

And Aaron. Complete unknown. Cooperative parents, says Conehead, who had him last year. I'm suspicious. Cooperative to this guy means the dad goes to construction sites in the middle of the night to swipe cones, and the mom stays in the truck keeping a lookout for the cops.

Vaughn is already in the books. His father, Mac, signed on to be my assistant. This will be our third year together.

Next, Trent, who has cystic fibrosis. Thick mucus builds up in his lungs and he has to take antibiotics to ward off infections. Noodle-sized arms and legs. Weighs only fifty-two pounds. Takes enzymes to help him digest food. Loves to run the bases, but tires easily. Lifespan will be seriously shortened unless there's a breakthrough. His parents mention the CF only when asked, as they want him to be treated the same as the other boys.

Trent called the night before tryouts and asked, pretty please, if he could be on my team, that he heard we have fun. He said his mother was getting ready to give him another stupid breathing treatment, and those things are easier to take with some good news.

I told him he could count on it.

He let out a roar.

And people wonder why a grown man would want to do this.

Finally, Walter. I graded him the lowest of any kid at tryouts. I also put a minus sign beside his name because he didn't seem to know his way around the field. The chief child-herder told him to go to the dugout and instead he went to the concession stand.

After the league director records my pick in Magic Marker—thus etching it in stone—I am advised Walter has never played a minute of baseball. Not pitching-machine league. Not T-ball. Not even a game of catch in the backyard.

Conehead says he sees Walter when he picks up his Jeff from after-school day care. "Kid loves dinosaurs. Brings action figures to lunch and trades them with the kindergartners."

Ah, yes. Welcome, Walter, to the Plaza Cubs. We won't be extinct for another three months yet.

The few days before the draft, I watched a television program about Little League baseball. The show's producers followed several teams in a hotly competitive Maryland league through the regular season and the post-season tournament. Managers, players, and parents wore microphones. The cameras even went inside league meetings.

It was ugly.

One coach had to be restrained from beating up an umpire. One parent had to be restrained from beating up a coach. Players taunted kids on opposing teams. Shouting matches between coaches were commonplace. Sometimes there was more arguing than playing.

I look around the room at the guys I'll be going up against in a few weeks.

Conehead gets a little intense sometimes, but he's not even in their league.

And the rest? Noncombatants, all. The only time you'd need to restrain anybody would be to keep him from going crazy laughing over Conehead's practice techniques.

There are several reasons for this.

- ✔ It's a must-play league, unlike some in the city. Sign up, write the check, sign the waiver, and your kid automatically makes the team. Mass participation has a way of sucking the blood out of veiny necks.
- ✔ It's a neighborhood league. Everybody knows everybody. Dads versus dads. You don't want to say or do something they'll be talking about over the backyard fence.
- ✔ These boys are only ten. It's hard to get into a good argument when the kid you're arguing about has Sweet Tarts on his breath.

Every kids' league has a few parents who get carried away. But the majority don't. They take the games for what they are—an opportunity to have an outing without issuing invitations. Forget the fussing and cussing that goes on in Maryland. Trust me. What gets said in our bleachers during games is much closer to reality.

Parent A, loudly, in direction of son: "You can do it. Give that ball a ride."

Parent A, under his breath: "He's going to strike out again, I just know it. We should have played soccer."

Small Child: "Mommy, can I sit in the dugout next to Paulie?"

Mother of Small Child: "No, you may not. The dugout is for players only."

Small Child: "But there's a dog in there. The dog doesn't play."

Mother, struggling to remain in control of the situation: "It's a retriever, dear. That's different."

Parent B, stunned: "He caught the ball! My son actually caught the ball!"

Parent C: "No, he didn't. The umpire signaled that he dropped it."

Parent B: "Whew! That's more like it. He had me going for a minute there."

Parent D, checking his watch: "How long are these games anyway? I've got to get back to work."

Parent E: "The coach hasn't gotten disgusted and sat on his clipboard yet. Another thirty minutes at least."

The evening's proceedings are almost over. All that's left is to listen to the league director's final instructions.

"For God's sake, guys, remember to pick up the bases after your game and lock them in the shed. Do you know how hard it is to order those things in mid-season? Remember, not all larceny is grand-theft auto.

"Every boy must have his own glove. It's the rules. Borrowing was for when we were kids.

"Designate someone to be in charge of the cashbox and lining up parents to work the concession stand. For best results, find a mom who's new to the league and has absolutely no idea what she's getting into. And tell your parents we need somebody to fix the popcorn popper and pronto. I turned it on last night, and it made noises you usually don't hear except under the hood.

"Make sure your catcher doesn't have a reaction to the face mask. I'm not kidding. Two years ago we had to call in a dermatologist.

"Be sure your players don't take the field with batting gloves on their throwing hands. I'm not kidding. Sometimes coaches from other leagues watch our games, and we don't want to be the butt of any more jokes than we are already.

"Finally, all players must wear protective cups. Helpful hint: In order to get maximum participation, encourage boys to thump them to the tune of 'Volga Boatman' or some other catchy chorus."

Nobody leaves until we check our equipment bags. Conehead suggests we inventory the contents to make sure we start with the same number of game balls and practice balls. He is looking right at me, and for good reason. It's a long season and, well, heh-heh, they have a way of disappearing.

A universal truth in youth baseball: You are going to lose some games, but you should never end the season in arrears on baseballs. The other coach may get the better of you in the field, but you can gain a measure of satisfaction by out-alerting him both during and after the game. In other words, making off with his baseballs.

The home team provides the two game balls and is awarded possession after the final out. But often the winning coach is in a celebratory mood and is slow to stake his rightful claim. I wait maybe five seconds, race to the pitching rubber, and add to our supply. If I'm caught, I say that after the thrashing we received, the least I can do is buff up the baseballs before returning them to their rightful owner.

As they say, winning isn't everything.

The good coach can usually make off with at least one of the enemy's infield balls during the game. My strategy is to hustle to my coaching position and engage one of the grown-ups on the other team in banal chitchat, all the while hoping for a stray return of the infield ball.

I have no chance at the ball the player tosses to the opening of the dugout, because that's where all the adults hang out. But it's another matter on an infield ball heaved lazily, well up the line, where there's only me and the yawning high school sophomore of an umpire. In the "Hey, batta, batta" excitement of the start of another inning, I sneak the thing into my pocket and no one is the wiser.

The Plaza Cubs might not win very many games, but our players will have their choice of batting practice balls.

3
NETTING SOME BACKYARD KIDS

It's the second day of school after the end of spring break. Traces of snow cling to the roots of the tree beside our trampoline. The players dive-bomb off the top branch. I learned long ago not to look.

Parents stick around for an informal meeting. I tell them practices will be about seventy-five minutes unless we start glove-slinging and, then, who knows. I tell them many sessions will be in the backyard because of the shortage of fields. I also make a point of emphasizing proper attire of baseball pants and baseball shoes, both for the sake of the game and in case one of the other coaches furtively drives by the house on a scouting mission.

If he sees we're all properly fitted, and none of us are playing with the dog, and none of us have our faces painted, that's news as devastating as if he observes me warming up the fourth-grade version of Randy Johnson.

I sit the kids down and go over a few rules.

No climbing the net. No saying things like "I saw your girlfriend naked." You will all be expected to get behind the plate during practice and no whining about it. No saying the words you see on the urinal at school.

OK to say you got hit in the balls or the privates or the cookies. Not OK to say "dickless in Seattle." "Pissed off" is OK. "Pecker" is out. So is "shit." So are double-entendre whispers about Uranus. Even if the other team's second baseman is a son of a bitch, you are to keep it to yourself.

OK to take a piss in the woods next to the trampoline. OK, I guess, to crap there, too. OK to practice some Stone Cold Steve Austin wrestling holds on a willing teammate. Not OK to act like Ricky Henderson.

The section of yard next to the batting net is filled with multicolored canvas bags containing all the players' baseball needs and then some. Danny, I notice, packs a cell phone. K. B., swimming goggles. Walter, doughnuts. Trent, his inhaler.

Mac, an industrial contractor by trade, comes early to inspect the batting net.

Actually, it's his net. It's just in my yard.

He furnished the support beams. And the posthole digger. And the leveler. He was the one who suggested we change the location of our holes after we struck a mother lode of a septic tank field. And the one with enough foresight to have a bar of Lava soap at the ready for his witless co-worker who allowed sewer matter to give him a facial.

In other words, I worked like someone who types for a living.

But the backstop was my creation. Hay bales. Stolen two by two under cover of darkness from an unsuspecting trailer park where they were being totally wasted on a ditch line.

I stacked them five abreast and the batting net was complete. A marriage of sport, the farm and the sea.

Mac takes Caleb, Graham, and Vaughn—the kids we see as having the best arms—off to one side for pitching practice.

I fashion a batting order and commence to being both hitting instructor and fat-pitch pitcher.

It's April, for goodness sake. Nibbling at the corners can wait until the concession stand orders hotdog buns.

The first time through the lineup is serious. Stride toward the mound, Evan. Extend your arms, Aaron. Don't be afraid, Trent. Don't swing until after I release the ball, Walter.

Then, some geography fun mixed in with learning how to get out of the way of the ball.

Me: "Adam, you're going down (baseball parlance for a pitch to the cranium area) unless you can answer the following question."

Adam, nonplussed: "OK."

Me: "You're supposed to be scared."

Adam: "I'm not."

Me, with big smile, realizing I stole one at the draft: "Name the largest city in Colorado."

Danny, loudly and in singsong voice: "Aw, that's easy. Why don't you ask me that?"

Me: "Be quiet. I'll throw at you later. Adam, do you know?"

Aaron: "No fair. Adam's probably from there."

Adam: "Am not."

Me: "There is no 'fair' in Going Down Game."

Felix: "Make him know the governor, too."

Me, diplomatically: "Knowing the largest city in Colorado is enough. Governor is for the people who live there."

Danny, bragging: "My mom knows the governor."

Evan: "You're lying. Shut up."

Danny: "Well, I'll bet she almost knows him."

Evan: "Danny, your cell phone is ringing."

Danny: "Shut up."

Me: "Time's up, Adam. What's the largest city in Colorado?"

Adam: "Uh, Salt Lake City."

Me, feigning delight at the blunder: "Wrong. Denver. You're going down."

I flip the next pitch inside. Adam casually ducks out of the way.

Me: "Who's next?"

All hands up.

I choose Danny.

Me, knowing who I'm up against and trying to think of a stumper: "OK, smart guy, where are the Pyrenees Mountains?"

Danny, almost instantly: "Spain."

Me, impressed: "Very good."

Danny, concerned: "Does this mean I won't be going down?"

Me: "Yes. You beat the game."

Danny: "I don't want to beat the game."

Pause for a few seconds.

Danny: "I'm changing my answer. Switzerland."

Me: "What do you mean, Switzerland?"

Danny: "That's where your mountains are."

Me: "No, they're not.

Danny: "I know that, but I want to play the game."

I've been through this kind of thing with him before. He'll badger me until the end of practice and maybe longer. The only alternative is to lob one high and tight, which I do.

Other boys on team, in loud voice: "Danny went down. Danny went down."

Danny, beaming that he has been made part of the group: "I know where the mountains are now. Egypt. C'mon, you know I'm wrong. Throw at me again. You promised."

Walter's turn. Like Danny, he has a strong desire to be

accepted by the other players. Unlike Danny, he is not a strong student.

The large child climbs in the net and stands squarely on home plate. I tell him to step back. He moves away so far that he couldn't reach the outside corner if he were hitting with a basketball player.

He's holding the bat wrong, his stance is terrible, and his oversized batting helmet gives the impression there's a small washtub on top of his head. These things will have to wait. Today I'll settle for getting him to stand the proper distance from the plate.

I start out pitching normally, but Walter doesn't make contact until my toss comes in at the same miles per hour as his age.

The other boys are quick to notice and I hear a few chuckles. I shoot them a hard glance and stop practice.

Walter is an equal member of our team, I lecture. We're all in this together, part and parcel, players and coaches. The quicker we as individuals can teach Walter to hit and catch, the better we will be as a whole.

One final hard glance and then it's back to practice.

Walking back to my position, I critique my first speech of the season. Good except for "part and parcel." Possible UPS connotation. Next time play it straight.

Walter steps back to the plate. Literally. I tell him that's enough for one day.

"I want to play Going Down," he says stubbornly.

Enough things haven't worked out today for this kid. He needs something good to happen. I select a question I save for just such emergencies.

"Walter, what is the largest city in New York State?"

He has no clue.

"Hint," I say. "Sounds the same."

Murmuring in background.

"Boston," Walter shouts.

Unfortunately, he chose to listen to Felix.

I decide we can get out of this without either of us losing face. I'll feed him one down the middle, he'll back out, and I'll praise his reflexes.

Unfortunately, I forget where he's standing. Down the middle to Walter is toward body parts. He uses his hand as a shield. Bad move. The ball bounces off his wrist and pops him in the jaw.

Two hurts in one play. First cry of the season.

And a good time to quit practice.

I announce that Evan and I are going to McDonald's and everybody is welcome.

The kids from last year knew this was coming and pile in. Felix, who suspected as much, gets permission. So does Caleb. Vaughn and Mac are set to follow.

Walter wants to come. His mother is hesitant. She's not so sure about this baseball business and, besides, he has homework.

"Look, Mom," he says excitedly as she gets out of the car. "I got popped."

She runs her fingers across the red mark on his face. I thought she might be upset with me, but she smiles. It's as if she knew something might happen.

"It doesn't hurt, though. Please. Please, can I go? I want to be with my team."

Her mouth moves but nothing comes out. Walter interprets that as a "yes," runs to my back seat, and climbs in.

The single mom is still not sure. Walter is her main squeeze and I'm just a stranger in a sweaty Cubs hat.

I tell her everything will be fine. I even suggest that she sneak in the rear of the parking lot after we've gone inside. This way, she's right there should she want to haul him off.

"No, you take him. Walter needs this. He's never been around other boys that much. Just don't be too late bringing him back."

He waves goodbye to her as I drive away. Clearly, he's never done anything like this in his life.

"Boy, we're gonna have fun," Walter says as he digs his knees into my back.

On the way, I tell Graham I'll give him a quarter if he can name two cities in Georgia.

"Atlanta" comes quickly.

A good deal of mumbling from the back seat.

Then, "Macon."

I give him his quarter.

Graham returns it, putting on his best Supreme Court Justice face.

"Evan told me. That would be cheating."

Felix tells Walter he can take off his batting helmet now.

The conversation in the car focuses on whether or not it's possible to stick a McDonald's Monopoly game piece back on a drink cup after it's been pulled off.

Graham: "You could, but they might arrest you."

Danny: "I was arrested once."

Evan: "You're lying."

Danny: "Well, my dad knows somebody who's been arrested."

Evan: "Idiot. He's a lawyer. That's his job."

Danny: "At least he has a job. You don't."

Evan: "Shut up."

Mac is like me in that he likes to set up situations with the boys that he knows will make us laugh out loud.

Tonight, it's paying for their own food. Most kids this age run to their seats, grab a bunch of straws, and let their parents sort out the dollars and cents. It's this not knowing how much things cost, Mac decides, that will provide the evening's entertainment.

He lines up the boys and gives each the money entrusted to us by their parents.

The food prices, Mac explains, are prominently displayed inside the restaurant. Add a little tax and make your order. If you overshoot the mark, it will teach you to add better next time.

"In other words, men," he announces, "you're on your own."

Mac and I order quickly and take our seats.

Showtime.

Much whispering. Then Walter nervously steps up to the counter, holding his money. Pointing to the burger bin, he says: "Four dollars' worth, please."

Mac and I turn our faces, not wanting the boys to see us cracking up.

Graham loves cheese. He asks the counter girl how many extra pieces of cheese he can get on his cheeseburger for his two dollars. She defers to the manager, who guesses ten.

Caleb takes the position that he's already had one math class today, and he's not about to do a bunch of extra ciphering in his off-duty time. He orders only large fries, confident it won't take an overbite out of his three dollars.

Danny asks why Caleb doesn't get more food since he hasn't eaten since noon.

"Not hungry."

"Aw, you are, too. You just can't add good in your head."

"Shut up."

Felix orders enough for two people. The total comes to ninety cents more than his allotment.

Danny comes to his rescue, and promptly announces that a ten-cent helper's fee will be tacked on to the principal and both are due next practice.

Then Danny asks the girl at the counter for a pen, does some quick math on a napkin, and figures out an assortment of food that comes closest to his five dollars without going over the actual amount.

"Get him on 'Price Is Right,'" Mac says, "and we'll all be rich."

Vaughn, who also has five dollars, borrows from Danny, but in a different way, one that doesn't require repayment.

"Make that two," he says, pointing to Danny's order and knowing he'll slide in under the limit.

I tell Mac he's outdone himself this time.

"Had the entire off-season to think about it."

Evan bolts his food and runs to the play area. Because he isn't paying attention, he trips over a kid's foot and runs into the side of the trash can. He brushes himself off and keeps going. This is his main athletic attribute. You can hit him in the head with a brick and he'll go on about his day.

I watch him go down the slide. I know he won't always be this way, but here's wishing.

A father couldn't hope for a better companion. Even disposition. Constant smile. Happy at whatever he's doing. I could take him to a three-hour meeting of the Zoning Board and he'd sit there patiently until it was time to leave.

Many times he forgets I'm more than four times his age.

It's "Dad, hurry up, you gotta see this. 'Animal Planet' is on and these birds are eating the elephant's crap like it's candy."

And: "Dad, on a scale of one to ten, grade me on this fart."

And: "Hey, Dad, what will you give me if I can flush one of my feet down the toilet?"

It's hard coaching your son. You can expect too much. You can expect too little. I think the best way is to pretend there's a video camera trained on your every move at games and practices. You must conduct yourself toward your son in such a way that you would not be ashamed to watch the unedited tape that night.

Last year we played fourteen games and had who knows how

many practices. I could watch most of the videotapes in good conscience. Yeah, I got too excited when our number nine guy got a big hit, and, yeah, I rooted them on so much in the Reds game that I lost my voice, and there was the pulled muscle I got running toward my third baseman after he caught a pop-up that clinched an upset victory. But nothing that would make me destroy a tape.

Except that one game.

We were playing a team I knew we could beat. Our guys had won only two games and this might be our last chance in the regular season.

Evan booted ground ball after ground ball at shortstop. When I put him at second, he dropped throw after throw when we had chances for forceouts.

The last error put the tying run on base.

I exploded. "What's the matter, Evan?" I screamed. "A two-year-old could have caught that ball."

My son looked at me. I looked at him. The line had been crossed and we both knew it. I was out of control.

The next batter struck out. We won the game, as if that mattered.

I ran onto the field and put my arm around Evan.

"What I did was totally stupid and totally uncalled for," I told him. "You have my word it will never happen again."

He forgives easily. The team had our usual victory celebration in the outfield, and he sat beside me the entire time. He showed I'm special to him.

From now on, I vowed, I'll return the favor. Dropped balls and all.

Walter sees a friend from school who asks him to join their table.

"Can't. I'm with my team. And you can't join until you know where the mountains are."

4

LEARNING TO PLAY A DECENT GAME OF CATCH

Class is in session.

Baserunning: Go halfway on fly balls. If you're on second, advance to third immediately on ball hit to right side. On ball hit to left side, wait until the shortstop or third baseman throws to first. No leading off until the ball has passed home plate. You have to slide on close plays or you can be called out. Thank the personal-injury lawyers for that one. Listen to me if you're on third base and the ball gets away from the catcher. It could bounce back toward the plate and you'll be an easy out. If you hit for extra bases, don't circle all the way to the outfield like half our players did in the nine-year-old league. If you find yourself at the same base with a teammate, it's high crimes and misdemeanors.

Defense: Ask yourself before each pitch what you'll do if the ball comes your way. Field ground balls in the center of your body. Use two hands to catch the ball. Practice catching and throwing all in one motion. The second baseman is cutoff man on balls hit to the right side. Shortstop handles center and left field. Second baseman covers first on a bunt. Third basemen, you have to go hard after every ball hit to your left because the shortstop will never be able to make the play. Outfielders, take a crow hop before throwing to a base. On a fly ball, make sure your first step is back. If you see interesting plant life you think your mother would like for her birthday, wait to pick it until after the game.

Ah, the outfield. No kid wants to play there.

So the good Minor League coach never ventures beyond this point without a prepared text.

Me: "Where does Ken Griffey play? Where does Sammy Sosa play? Where does Larry Walker play?"

Them: "Outfield."

Me: "They're all great players, aren't they?"

Them: "Yes."

Me, building to climax: "Where would a team be without outfielders?"

Danny: "They wouldn't win very many games, and the players would get mad because they wouldn't get their performance bonuses."

Me: "That's right. Every position is important and the outfield is no exception."

Graham, pointing to right field: "I know a kid who peed there in T-ball."

Me: "If you don't pay attention in the outfield, what's going to happen?"

Walter: "You won't make a goal?"

Me: "That's soccer. Their field is across the street. This is baseball."

Felix: "You get hit in the head by a fly ball."

Me: "Exactly. And how do we keep that from happening?"

Evan: "Get good enough so you don't have to play there."

I decide to revisit this topic later in the preseason.

Danny is concerned about a reading assignment and asks if he can call the school. This is a first for me: One of my players sitting on third base, cradling a cell phone and writing notes from the homework hotline on a legal pad.

Prediction: Minor League, year 2008. Laptops in the dugouts.

Mac and I pair off the kids and have them throw to each other. Forget what they do in the batting cage. This is when you find out about your team. If your guys can't play a decent game of catch, you're doomed to the second division.

Of the boys I've had before, Graham does this the best. Good hand-eye coordination plus an athletic ability that's well above average.

Felix, a sidearmer, should be able to play some first base. May be able to pitch some if I can teach him the concepts of forceouts and covering home on a passed ball.

When Evan concentrates and throws overhand, he can wing it with any of them. But let him get the least bit lazy with his motion and the ball is liable to go anywhere. I know. Our woods are alive.

Vaughn is our beefiest player. A hard thrower, but slow to react on balls he has to reach for.

Danny has the weakest arm of any kid I've ever coached. Put it this way: Let him pitch to a seven-year-old team from the Pyrenees, and they'd blast him all over the lot.

K. B. misses a lot of balls. Then it takes him forever to throw.

Walter sticks his glove out in rigid fashion in the manner of a school-crossing guard extending her warning sign. Snares maybe one in three. Throws like the word my former youth-league baseball coaches—unenlightened, to a man—used to refer to a female person.

Trent has a nice throwing motion. He's afraid of the ball, though, and always catches off to the side.

Aaron, a lanky kid with long arms, shows above-average skills, but struggles to keep his emotions in check. Shows his disappointment when a throw goes awry or a ball sails over his webbing. Heaves glove in anger after one particularly dismal catch. We have a talk.

Caleb is everything I remember last year from the nine-year-old league. Catches effortlessly. Throws to the same spot almost every time. Can anyone say "shortstop"?

Adam, one of our bigger boys, has a decent arm but catches awkwardly. And badly. Two balls bounce off his shin, but he says nothing. Doesn't even rub it. I like him already.

Infield drill.

Half the boys at shortstop and the rest at first. Who can catch a ground ball, plant and throw? Who can catch it without getting knocked back to the fence?

Outfield drill.

Half the boys playing short man and the rest in normal position. Who can catch over his shoulder? Who can move up and back?

Baseballs are flying everywhere for the first time in eight months. This is great.

Time for the find-a-third-baseman drill.

Evan and Graham catching. Half the kids grab helmets and take turns as baserunners at second. The rest alternate playing third. Mac shows them how to take throws from catcher with feet straddling the bag to tag out the sliding runner. I bounce a ball off the backstop, which is the runner's signal to advance. Evan or Graham retrieves the ball and heaves it to third. The idea is to catch it cleanly and, in one motion, make the tag. This isn't easy at this level. Third base is the sixth most important position to fill after pitcher, catcher, shortstop, first and second, and pickings get slim. Opposing coaches study this position with the intensity of carnivores. If the kid you have there can't catch, it's open season on stealing third.

A few poker-faced Minor League coaches of my acquaintance have been known to compensate for a lack of talent at this position by pulling a bluff.

One way is to instruct your third baseman to chatter incessantly and pound the pocket of his glove for all it's worth to give the false impression he's really good, and that a runner intent on taking liberties is making the mistake of his young life.

Another strategy is for the coach to holler this at his third sacker: "OK, kid, you've tagged out six guys in a row trying to steal third. What say we go for the league record?"

Mac and I soon have our coachspeak in midseason form.

"Vaughn, it's legal to bend your back when catching the ball."

"Walter, don't stick your glove out like that until you make sure nobody's face is there."

"Danny, pretend the ball is a letter and you're trying to deliver it as soon as possible."

"Relax, Aaron, nobody's perfect."

"K. B., do what you're doing but twice as fast."

"Evan, we are absolutely not going to lose a ball this season during fielding practice. Throw another one in the weeds and run three laps."

Mac and I review what to do on rundowns and then we end practice with some glove-slinging.

Word of my cash giveaway program gets around. Caleb and Trent ask if I'll give them a dollar for catching my best Major League pop-up.

"I don't have to ask for my allowance," Aaron reasons. "I'll just go to baseball practice."

Danny asks to keep a practice ball that's come undone. He says he wants to dissect it.

Adam's dad introduces himself. Chemical engineer. Born in India. Came to this country to go to college. No desire to go back. Krishna asks in slightly broken English if Adam has been any trouble.

I say no, that I wish I had ten more just like him.

You just tell me, Krishna insists, and it won't happen again.

I do my best to reassure him. Adam, I say, is just great.

Krishna talks about growing up poor. There was no time back then for sports, he says. "You had to have some kind of job by the time you were eight to help support the family. My money went for bread and milk."

He says he doesn't want Adam to miss out on being a little boy the way he did. "This baseball, I don't know very much. But I'm going to learn and I want Adam to learn."

He picks up a bat as if to check for molecular structure. "The only way I know how to do something is go at it hard. When I was this age, the other boys in the school made fun of how I had to work all the time. I used that to push myself. Every time something rough came up in America, I would pretend people were saying I couldn't do it, and that made me try that much more. I want to teach Adam this way. But this is a new time, and I just don't know. Do you think I'm right?"

I only met this guy three minutes ago and already he's asking me the secret to life.

"Uh, yeah, sure," I reply as I pick up the equipment. I cannot summon the philosophical depth necessary to give this question the attention it deserves while watching Evan get his glove on in time to catch the ball after crawling through Trent's legs.

"But I'm not serious all the time," Krishna says, smiling. "I make jokes. You'll see."

K. B. and Aaron need rides home. I take the long way with Aaron, hoping to find out why the boy is so hard on himself. I learn that his stepfather is unemployed and his mother works at a discount department store. They live in another school district ten miles away. Aaron says they've moved three times in the last two years.

He tells me his grandmother paid the league fee and bought his glove, a good deed she repeated for Aaron's stepbrother, Winston, who's a year younger. "Winston's not like me. He's good," Aaron says. "He hit four home runs last year and made the traveling team."

I tell Aaron he can be a good player, too.

"No, I can't. Everything I do on the baseball field comes out bad."

I want to continue our little talk, but the subject turns to video games.

K. B. casually mentions that he has a Sony PlayStation, a Nintendo 64, and a Sega Saturn.

Aaron can't believe it. "Three? Just for you? You don't have to share?"

I'm not surprised. The guy who coached him last season told me he never saw K. B. wear the same clothes twice, and that he was always playing with a new game system.

The conversation moves to swimming pools. K. B. has one in his backyard. So does Danny.

"I don't even know anybody who has a pool," Aaron says. "Aren't they a lot of trouble?"

"Not if you have a pool man," K. B. replies off-handedly.

Aaron wants to know what such a person does.

K. B. explains.

"That doesn't sound very hard," Aaron says. "Why don't you let me be your pool man and I could swim for free?"

We come to Aaron's neighborhood, one of rundown houses and mobile homes. K. B. is quiet. This might be the first time he's come in direct contact with poor people.

Aaron points me down the bumpy street that's littered with discarded diapers and plastic soda bottles. "This is it right here."

I stop outside a small house trailer that's missing the front step. Toys are strewn on top of a dented roof. Winston and a little girl are looking out a dirty window.

"Thanks for the ride. I'll try to come to the next practice, but I might not be able to if our car's still in the shop."

I tell him to call and I'll pick him up.

"You'd do that?"

I nod.

"Hey, all right." He puts on a happy face, the first one I've seen.

I take K. B. home in silence.

He's seen another world.

And maybe been given something to think about.

Back to Mac's house for a coaches' meeting, meaning we put away a few beers and talk about the coming season.

But first we rekindle a running argument which can be reduced to a statement and a rebuttal.

"I can strike you out."

"No, you can't."

I have a pretty good arm for a typist. I can throw batting practice for an hour without getting tired and without plunking a little kid. I can stand in right field on the high school diamond and throw one-hoppers to the catcher. And then, of course, there's my ability to throw a baseball high enough to engage in glove-slinging.

Most of the dads get a load of all this and are in at least a degree of awe, saying their arms would fall right off if they tried that. I have grown to appreciate the compliments, and even look forward to them. I might not be able to build anything, but at least I can throw like a seventh-grade version of Sammy Sosa.

Mac didn't say anything the first night we met. He just took the ball and threw it higher. Then he stood in right field and threw home like Sammy did when he was a senior in high school.

Still unwilling to concede best-arm honors to an assistant coach, I bought one of those radar balls that gives you a readout when it smacks into the mitt. I couldn't top sixty-one miles per hour, even with two leg kicks and a crow hop. Mac got up to sixty-seven, but he threw a couple of low ones and our accountant of a catcher called a halt, saying he wanted his ankles to be able to go to work the next day.

Speed doesn't matter, I countered. Strikeouts do.

So Mac and I spent the end of several on-field practices trying to throw the ball by each other. Kids were outfielders and foul-ball chasers. Dads cheered lustily as we took turns squinting into the moonlight. Moms wrote us off as a couple of idiots.

The results were inconclusive. I lost more balls, but Mac rolled more under cars.

He claims he K'd me one night, but I swear I foul-tipped the third strike.

Looking back, I'd have to amend that to say I foul-tipped something. In the gloaming, it could have been the car keys Mac's wife threw at me to signal she was past ready to go home.

The popcorn finally ready, we review our roster:

Graham—Ask him to come to McDonald's after practice and he'll politely say, "Yes, if I'm allowed." Our only buzz-cut blond. Afraid of lightning. Takes trombone lessons. Asks his father to sign him up for distance races, not because he's a good runner, but because he wants to build up endurance. Went through period of depression following car accident. Starting to come out of it. Says he wants to be a big-league baseball player.

Evan—In gymnastics since he was four. Has taken a lot of spills in that sport, and, as a result, it takes a lot to hurt him or make him afraid. Has a lot of upper-body strength, which translates into good bat speed. Can stand in against the eighty-mile-per-hour machine at Two-Bit Sports and put the bat on the ball. Far from a gifted athlete, though. Will only be decent at a sport if he practices. Even smaller than Danny. Stubborn. I almost called the Guinness people to see if they have a category for "Boy Who Took the Longest to Be Toilet-Trained."

Felix—Probably our fastest runner. Lives near field and skateboards to practice. Does well when he can rely on instinct. Struggles when he has to process data quickly, as in determining which base to throw to. Cute lisp. Cuter mumble. Says he wants to be a pirate when he grows up.

Danny—Despite limited ability, has high desire to play. Pesters his parents, who know little about the game, to sign him up for baseball camps. If parents are in chambers, doesn't hesitate to ask me to take him to games. By far the smartest boy on the team. Wants to be a systems analyst for NASA when he grows up. Runs like a penguin.

Caleb—Will probably average walking one man or less per inning, which is excellent for our league. Will sulk if there's a team outing and he doesn't get to go. Wants to be an actor when he grows up.

K. B.—Mac noticed the same "slo-mo" thing I did. He says it's like the boy takes a victory lap without picking up the victory first. He dispenses high-fives and hand slaps to teammates even after routine plays, and insists on receiving same. We decide we have one of a new breed, an ESPN player. A kid who spends hours and hours watching sports on TV, paying particular attention to his favorite players' post-play antics. He picks up on the home-run trot more than the good swing, and the flashy way Ken Griffey, Jr., goes stylin' after a fly ball more than the actual catching technique. Convince K. B. that our field doesn't have an eye in the sky, Mac says, and we should be all right.

Walter—There's no give-up in this boy. Despite what may prove to be a permanent inability to hit. Despite having three of Vaughn's throws knock his glove completely off. Leads team in saying, "Did I do good?" Leads team in asking, "When are we going to verse the Dodgers? I've got two friends on that team."

Adam—Outstanding work ethic. Has already had one private session at the batting net and wants another before season starts. Dad depends on him to know the practice schedule. If he misses one or is late, he has to run laps around the subdivision.

Aaron—Will make an excellent play one minute and then do something boneheaded the next. Our only player who spits before batting. Tells me he once ate four dollars worth of Reese's Cups without throwing up.

Trent—Steps in bucket on any pitch even remotely inside. Sometimes gets in arguments with other boys. Has been picked on a lot for being small, and this is his way of firing the first shot. Dad says doctors might not let Trent play if he keeps losing weight.

Vaughn—With his size, potentially one of our better hitters. Second only to Graham in saying "Excuse me" and "Thank you." With his arm, potentially one of our better pitchers. Says "stanima" for "stamina." Favorite thing to do is sit on riverbank fishing and watching the world go by. In an all-star game last year, he was so quiet on the bench the coach thought he was sick and didn't put him in.

Mac shakes his head. We've had this conversation about his son before.

"He's just so passive about everything. School, church choir, baseball, the Scouts—whatever he's doing, all he does is show up. I wish I could get him excited about something. Anything."

We've tried hard with baseball.

In a game last year, he pitched a one-hitter and struck out fourteen. His teammates went crazy over him. So did their parents, saying this had to be the second coming of Nolan Ryan. I pronounced him the player of the day and treated him to all he could eat at Dairy Queen.

This is something to build on, Mac said at the time.

His next start was against one of the better teams. All week we pumped Vaughn up, telling him how valuable he is to the team and how we were going to need his very best effort to win the next one.

Vaughn got knocked out in the first inning. A bunch of hard hits, a bunch of walks, and a slow roller up the middle that he didn't give much chase to. When I went to the mound to take him out, he didn't seem disappointed in his performance, or angry, or relieved that the ordeal was over. He just stood there looking at me.

"He's a good boy, Mac," I say, speaking what both of us know is the truth.

"Yeah," Mac replies, his voice trailing off. "Maybe this will be the year."

Evan's enjoyment of baseball is directly linked to when he first started catching. When I had him at second, he rarely talked about playing and seldom watched a game on TV. The game on the field, he told me, is too slow.

Toward the end of last year's season, our regular catcher took a foul ball off the toe. The nail was cut and blood seeped into his socks.

He was my only boy who demonstrated any catching aptitude. Look, I told him. We can make some noise in the tournament, but we've got to be solid behind the plate. Whatever you do, don't show the sock to your mother.

Two hours later, I got a call.

He showed the sock to his mother.

Third base, she said, sounds about right.

She was team mom and keeper of the cashbox and her husband rewired the scoreboard.

I had no choice. There would be a change of personnel at the hot corner.

So who to put behind the plate?

I talked with Evan about it later that night. There was no mincing of words.

A hard foul ball off the catcher's mask probably feels like missing your horizontal-bar routine in gymnastics and your face going splat on the mat.

But look on the bright side, I went on. When you brag about getting hurt at gym, most people don't know what you're talking about. When you say you got hurt catching, they'll know exactly.

Sounds good, he said.

So I pulled a Coach-Daddy and started him back there in our next game. He missed more balls than he caught, and the other team ran the bases like wild horses.

But he took a newfound interest in the game and showed steady improvement. When he wasn't showing me where a ball hit his finger, he was memorizing the stats of his favorite players and taping Major League games he didn't have a chance to watch that night.

Suddenly we share the same passion. It's been great. We talk baseball in the enjoyment of each other's company, and our relationship couldn't be stronger. The unfitting gear drapes over him like one of Drew Carey's sweaters, but he's happy. So am I. Sue me. Evan's our catcher.

Caleb on the mound should be a big key early in the season when so many games are decided by walks. He won't dominate like a Joey, but he'll throw it over the plate. The hitting takes a few weeks to kick in. We should pick up some wins in April we might not get in June. Graham will be our second starter. He'll also back up Caleb at shortstop.

Vaughn and Felix are our most likely first basemen.

Danny is a natural at second. He'll never make an errant toss because that's as far as he can throw. If K. B. plays the infield, it will have to be here until we can do something about his slo-mo.

Aaron should be our third baseman, but Adam has a better attitude and a better work ethic and is getting better every day. Felix could get a look here, too.

Walter has right field all to himself. Trent is good on grounders and decent on flies. He'll probably start in left. We'd love to have a good ball-chaser in center, but that means robbing from the infield. Graham could play here against teams with above-average hitting. Against the rest, maybe we can slide by with K. B., Aaron, or Felix.

It's early yet, but I ask Mac to suggest a batting order. He has Evan leading off and then Graham, Caleb, Vaughn, Felix, K. B., Aaron, Adam, Danny, Trent, and Walter.

I disagree with where he put Walter. True, he's our worst hitter, but he's also slow and a poor baserunner. I'd rather put a quicker player in the last slot—even if he can't hit—so as not to clog the bases for the top of the order.

I also like batting Danny higher. He doesn't hit the ball as much as he pokes at it, but most of his poking is to the left side where the infielders have a longer throw. By the time the ball gets to first, Danny could scale the Pyrenees.

Speaking of hitting, Mac tells me what happened after one of Conehead's batting practices.

"Joey hit some balls to the parking lot on the church field. Conehead wanted to find out how far they went, so guess what he did?"

"Stepped off the distance?"

"Nope. He left one of his pylons at the point of impact, and then went to see a friend who's a surveyor. They brought back some equipment and took an official measurement—182 feet, 6 inches."

I shake my head. Next he'll have his pitchers throwing to a plumb bob.

5

THROWING HOTTERS AND VISITING THE ACTORS' STUDIO

The field is a quagmire, so I move practice to the netless tennis court beside the middle school.

We continue our efforts to have a good game of catch. Follow through on your throws, I say. Aim at the other guy's chest. Watch the ball into your glove. Don't back up. Pretend the glove is an extension of your hand.

But mostly we're here to have fun.

Home Run Derby.

Game. Set. Match.

Adam and Aaron are captains and they choose up sides. I pitch the rubber ball that used to be a baseball until I mowed over it in the batting net.

No sliding, I tell the boys, and no throwing those expensive bats on the hard surface. Ball under the fence is two bases. Over the fence is a four-bagger, and you may mildly chide the opposition on your home-run trot. Anything hit in the ad court is foul.

The reduced-pain chemistry of the ball makes a huge difference.

Aaron keeps his front foot in and hits a couple of solid grounders. Walter still strikes out, but at least he gets around on it before the catcher throws the ball back. Danny actually swings hard instead of using the bat as a boxer would a right jab.

Mac serves as hitting coach.

"Evan, don't beat down on the ball. Swing level."

"Graham, you're taking too many strikes over the outside corner. Lean into the pitch."

"Vaughn, you're letting the ball jam you. Get your hands moving sooner."

Caleb is the first to go yard, a shot to straightaway center.

A large black dog runs up on the ball and assumes possession. Sharp teeth and a tongue the size of the pitching rubber are all over it like Roger Clemens on a .150 hitter. The owner appears. There's only one thing for me to say.

"Mister, can I have my ball back?" I may be far removed from my playing days, but I still remember the words.

Returning to the tennis court, I make the mistake of saying the ball has more than a little slobber on it.

K. B.: "I'm not batting with that nasty thing."

Aaron: "You wouldn't hit it anyway."

K. B.: "Shut up."

Danny: "I'll put my tongue on the ball if you give me a dollar, and I don't care if I get infected."

His parents go to Europe the way I go to the lake. Yet Danny would have them use their financial resources to provide long-term medical care for their only son. And for a reward equal to a large pack of LemonHeads.

Me: "Where's your sense of pride?"

Danny, starting to grab the ball: "Where's your dollar?"

Graham: "This is sick."

Trent: "What if somebody pukes on it? How much money would you want then?"

Danny: "That depends."

Evan: "What do you mean, depends? Puke is puke."

Danny: "If somebody is nice, then his puke isn't so bad."

Evan: "Who on the team is nice?"

Danny: "Certainly not you."

Me, realizing this won't come to an end on its own: "OK, OK, that's enough. Nobody's going to lick a dirty ball. Let's get back to the game."

K. B., still hesitant: "Wipe it off first."

I use the bottom of my shirt.

K. B.: "Now spray it."

Vaughn hits a home run. So does Graham. The middle of our lineup looks like it's going to have some pop.

Mac is showing Trent how much power he's losing by stopping his swing, when we hear a voice.

"Hey, can I play?"

It's Krishna, and in full Saturday afternoon attire. Madras shirt. Blue socks. Red shorts extending almost all the way to black shoes, revealing maybe two inches of knees.

"I've been practicing. Which team do you want me to go?"

Adam agrees to take his dad.

"But we hit better. You'll have to bat last."

He nods. Rookies know their place.

Krishna comes up with two runners on. He is bent over more than any hitter I've ever seen. His shirt becomes a canopy of shade for the catcher.

The combination of stance and clothing prompts me to lob the ball as I would to a nearsighted seven-year-old. Krishna hammers it over the fence. I stop the game.

"OK, slugger, try this one."

I serve one up the same way I would to Graham or Evan.

Another jack.

Krishna taps his bat. Then he points to center field, calling his shot à la Babe Ruth. "My wife bought me a baseball history book last week," he explains. "Let's go. Throw."

I give him a fast ball worthy of a twelve-year-old.

Gone.

"Simple engineering," Krishna says, grinning. "Bat creates force field."

I tell him to slide-rule this next pitch. Winding up like I'm going to throw a buzz ball, I deliver the cruelest offering an adult pretending to be a kid will ever see. A change-up.

The result is the Cecil B. DeMille of whiffs. Only the asphalt surface kept Krishna from becoming a human rivet.

I laugh until I cry.

"That's just strike one," he says, bending over still farther. "Throw me your best hotter."

The boys correct him. "Heater!"

"Whatever. You pitch. I hit."

I give him another change-up. Krishna's torque could power up a DC-10. Again I have him riveted.

"Good thing the two of you aren't married," Mac hollers. "This is physical cruelty if I've ever seen it."

Krishna taps his bat again. If I give him another change-up, he'll hit it over the black dog's head. So I slip in a fastball.

He's just now starting his swing. "No fair. You're not pitching what I'm thinking."

Adam tells his dad there's no "fair" in Home Run Derby.

Krishna Ruth doesn't get another one out of the infield the rest of the game.

"We do this again," he says, tucking in his shirt. "See, I like to make jokes."

Trent still steps out, even with the rubber ball. His dad

patiently tells him to believe in himself and keep his feet still. Trent says he's going to do better, only to bail out again upon first glimpse of the ball. His skin is a funny color. Trent's not saying, but I'm sure he doesn't feel good.

After the last home run, I play Box Game with the boys who are left. I put two gloves about fifteen feet apart, and tell them they are responsible for fielding all grounders and line drives within this space. They toss me the ball as they would in Pepper, and I spray it to their right or left.

Catch ten in a row, I explain, and you retire undefeated.

The other boys get to seven or eight and I purposely send one out of reach.

Trent has had enough bad things happen to him. It's time for something good. I keep every ball within easy range. He is the only player who gets to ten. The other kids don't suspect a thing.

"Dad, Dad," Trent shouts. "I was the bestest at the game."

Caleb goes with Evan and me for hamburgers. Between bites, I ask about this acting business.

"I like it. You make a lot of money, and you get to fool people all the time and not just at Halloween."

I get an idea that can help determine if Caleb has a shot at central casting. "Actors have to be able to think on their feet, right?"

He nods.

"Even more important, they have to say their lines with people looking on who might think they're crazy, right?"

Continued agreement.

"So I've come up with a little test for you. There's a Rand McNally book in my car. You know what that is, right?"

Caleb does.

"Here's what we do. I'll stop at a convenience store. You give Evan and me a few seconds to get situated and then you walk in.

You're clutching that book and you look very confused. With a straight face, you tell the clerk your father sent you in to find the small town of Rand McNally on the map. You tell him you have relatives there who are expecting you, and you're sure it's somewhere near Evansville, and you'd like to get there before nightfall. If you're a good actor, the clerk will bust his butt to find a place that's actually a map company."

Caleb shows keen interest in the game, but wonders one thing.

"What are you and Evan going to be doing all this time?"

"Do you actually think we'd miss something like this?"

Caleb practices his lying, first with Evan as the clerk and then with me. I'm impressed. No way Jim Carrey was this good at age ten.

Like a thief casing his bank, we cruise by convenience stores. One clerk is busy with her fingernails, and probably not in the mood to help a lost little boy. Another looks like a graduate student who might catch on to what we're doing. A Shell station looks perfect. A bored clerk who's reading a Sidney Sheldon novel.

Evan and I take our positions at stage right by the breath mints.

Act one, Scene one: Freckle-faced little boy enters store with map book. He has a cut on a leg from where he disobeyed his coach's instructions not to slide on the tennis court.

Kid, pathetically: "Mister, we're lost. My dad has relatives in Rand McNally, Indiana, and I know that's somewhere near here, and we're supposed to be there in time for dinner, and now they're going to be all mad at us. You live around here. Could you please find Rand McNally on this map?"

Clerk, who obviously has never even heard of graduate school: "Rand McNally, Indiana? Town doesn't ring a bell. Hey, Clarence, can you help us?"

Clarence, stacking Vienna Sausages in the front aisle: "I've probably been there once or twice, but I'm not much good at directions."

Clerk: "Let me see that book. Maybe this Rand McNally place is so small it's not listed."

He runs his finger over the length and breadth of Southern Indiana.

"There's a Ramsey and a Milltown, but no Rand McNally. Are you sure it's not a county?"

Caleb, trying to cut the game short before he goes into hysterics: "Thanks for trying, mister. I'll go back to the car. Maybe my dad has figured it out by now."

Clerk, not ready to concede defeat: "Maybe it's a subdivision. They're always giving subdivisions strange names."

Clarence, dropping crate: "Send him to the arcade up the street. They know a lot about geography."

I buy some breath mints and a Twinkie. The least I can do is patronize the store after such a stellar performance by an unwitting supporting cast.

Evan says we played Caleb's game. Now it's time to play his.

He has me drive to the still-soggy outfield. "I just invented it," Evan explains. "You throw the ball so we have to dive for it, and then you say which one of us had the most spectacular catch."

I ask what he calls this new game.

He gives me an exasperated look. "Duh. Spectacular Catch."

Caleb is more graceful going after the ball, but has more of an aversion to getting filthy. Evan is not as quick and he jumps off the wrong foot, but he loves ruining his clothes. The game becomes hotly competitive.

Evan: "Caleb didn't dive for the ball. Tell him he's got to dive."

Caleb: "I can catch it without diving. I don't want to have mud in my nose like Evan."

Me: "Why don't you try diving a little bit and maybe Evan won't rag you so much?"

Caleb: "Do you have a blanket in your car?"

Me: "Why? You cold?"

Caleb: "No, to put on the field so I won't get dirty when I hit the ground."

Evan: "Don't be a pussy."

Me: "Caleb, even if I had a blanket I wouldn't spread it in center field."

Evan, after ripping out a section of sod with his face in the process of making the catch: "That's one for the highlight show."

Caleb, not impressed: "Funny, I don't see anybody filming."

Evan: "You're a pussy."

Caleb: "Shut up."

6
HITTING EACH OTHER UP

Time for kids to practice hitting against other kids.

It's much less frightening to bat against an adult—even if the adult throws harder—because the boys trust the adult to have pinpoint accuracy. They also know that should the adult nail them, their moms and dads can go to court and have the poor sap's assets obliterated.

A 10-year-old pitcher may or may not know where his ball is going. But should he hit you, it's considered part of the game and not a legal matter.

Evan volunteers to catch, the only boy to do so. Graham would rather pitch or play shortstop, and the rest of the kids have seen enough baseball games to know that a catcher might not end the season with the same cookie mix he had at the beginning.

A pathological exaggerator since he could talk, Evan actually hopes he does get hurt so he can go on and on about being in agony.

As final preparation for getting ready to hit against hurlers who also raise their hands for the lunch count, I decide to run through the batting order once more with me on the hill.

Which sets up the season's first game of Money Ball.

Each kid is issued a Dixie Cup with his name on it. Ten swings. Fifteen cents for a line drive. Dime for putting the ball in play. And five bucks for any ball hit back up the middle that causes me to go to the hospital. The catcher collects 75 cents for general principles.

I take nominations for banker, the person in charge of the Pringles can full of change.

This person, I explain, must be uncommonly honest. The rest of you will be busy hitting. This kid must be trusted to keep track of your good hits. He also must be trusted to put the proper coinage in the proper cup.

I mention that because last season a kid knocked the crap out of the ball and ended up with barely enough money to jingle because the banker got him confused with a teammate who couldn't have gotten a hit off Dear Abby.

Walter nominates himself.

"I'm not going to get any money, and this way I at least get to touch it."

Danny is quick to follow.

"I can beat the fifth-grade math teacher at chess. Need I say more?"

Danny is our banker.

Vaughn slams one to the back of the net and I holler for the Federal Reserve to dispense a quarter.

Aaron only makes contact on two pitches and they're weak foul balls. He throws his bat. We have a talk.

Walter has taken to holding his bat almost parallel to the

ground with the idea that maybe the ball will hit it. Mac takes him off to the side.

K. B. lacks bat speed, and the few balls he hits are little dribblers. He tells me his dad has bought a portable hitting machine that spits out plastic golf balls. I don't doubt that he's been practicing, but the way he looks now it'll be the middle of the season before he gets a high-five.

Adam continues to impress, not for hitting the ball as much as his lack of fear.

"The worst thing that can happen is that I'll have to go to the doctor, and I've been there before," he says, shrugging shoulders.

Caleb rips one that he thinks should be worth 15 cents, but I award only 10. He pouts and misses the next three pitches on purpose. We have a talk.

Graham doesn't hit any ball hard, and isn't happy about it.

"If I was as good as my dad, I'd be the best player on the team," he says, breaking into a refrain I heard several times last year.

He reaches in his back pocket and pulls out a baseball card of a very serious young man holding a big bat.

"That's him on his pro team," Graham says proudly. "You just know he's getting ready to bust one."

Trent sends the last two pitches a few feet in front of the plate. I pronounce them timely hits and order the banker to compensate him accordingly.

Caleb is warmed up and ready. Stay long enough, I announce to the other players, and you'll get a chance to pitch. Hit two guys and we'll put in someone else. Same for walking two in a row. Each hitter gets one regulation at-bat off each pitcher.

Mac dumps fresh change into the Pringles can, and says henceforth all Money Ball payouts will double.

He and I stand cross-legged behind the net with hands under our chins the way we've seen big league hitting instructors do on television.

If you weren't there:

- ✔ Caleb goes through nine batters and allows only one hit. He doesn't walk anybody and faces only one three-ball count. If he's acting, he's playing Greg Maddux.
- ✔ K. B. refuses to catch. We have a talk.
- ✔ Vaughn throws the hardest, but is also the wildest, quickly walking his limit.
- ✔ Evan loudly announces that it won't break his heart if he hits somebody. He says Vaughn gave him a seamer last year and he wants revenge.
- ✔ Walter fouls a pitch off Danny.
- ✔ Danny hits a pitch into Walter.
- ✔ Vaughn says he's sorry for the seamer and wants my personal guarantee Evan won't hit him. I tell him Evan doesn't throw all that hard and that should the worst happen, Mac has major medical. Thus reassured, he ducks under two pitches and then whistles a line drive.
- ✔ Graham fires a pitch that gets stuck in a hay bale. When catcher Caleb pulls it out, hundreds of black bugs pour out. Panic ensues. Practice is suspended and Raid sprayed until the backyard smells like it's been crop-dusted.
- ✔ The only thing slower than K. B.'s windup is his leg kick. A hitter could outgrow his bat waiting to swing.
- ✔ I have Danny and Walter wear batting helmets while pitching so they don't get killed. Memo to league president: Got any full-body armor?

Evan hits Aaron and Felix. Enough target practice for one day. A good time to go over signs.

Me: "Touching the ear is the indicator. That means what follows counts. If I don't touch my ear first, nothing is on and it doesn't matter what I do. Everybody got that?"

Danny: "Why don't we change the indicator every inning like they do in the big leagues?"

Me: "Because I'd get confused. Remember, I scored less than 1,000 on my SATs."

Danny: "If we get way ahead, will you let me coach third and change the signs every inning?"

Me: "Yes. Guys, let that be an incentive for you. Get 15 runs ahead and Danny gets to coach third."

Evan: "Danny wants to pretend he's signaling planes at the airport." Extends left hand straight up and right hand straight out. "This means park."

Danny: "Shut up."

Me, touching ear and then touching leg: "This is steal. Understand?"

Danny: "Any part of the leg? What about the hip?"

Graham: "My hip is part of my leg. Maybe your body is different, I don't know."

Danny: "Shut up."

Me, touching ear and then touching arm: "This means bunt. Leg is run. Arm is bunt. That's about as simple as it can get."

Mac: "Be sure you pay attention. In the pros, the manager might fine a guy $100 for missing a sign."

Trent: "Couldn't they get their dads to pay it?"

Most of the parents have gathered in the driveway. I go over a few rules.

No friends on other teams in dugout. No little brother or sister in dugout. No Virtual Pets in dugout.

Players aren't to eat hotdogs during game. Players aren't to visit with family members during game. Players aren't to drink from another player's water bottle unless they're best friends.

No sneaking earthworms into a teammate's bat bag. No putting done-with chewing gum on back of catcher's mask. And, above all, no giving opposing coaches any of our baseballs.

I field no question more substantial than Felix's uncle wanting to know if he should buy one of those new $160 bats from the sports store, or just go to Wal-Mart.

I suggest he assume Felix is a discount hitter until he proves otherwise.

Graham's dad sticks around after the other parents leave. I tell him about the baseball card that was passed around today at batting practice.

"Does he still have that old thing? My goodness."

Ken was a medium-round draft pick by the real Cubs as a first baseman. He had one decent season in the low minors before hurting his back. He couldn't hit the ball over the fence any more and was released midway through his second year.

But in Graham's eyes, his daddy was a big-leaguer. Last year, he told the other boys Ken hit six triples in spring training.

Not true. His dad wasn't even invited to camp.

Graham also told the other boys his dad was close personal friends with Ryne Sandberg and Rick Sutcliffe.

Not true. His dad never even met them.

Judging by what happened at the net, I tell Graham's dad it looks like we're in for another season of Story Time.

"I don't know why he does that," says Ken, whose short-lived baseball career might as well have been in another life. Now he's turned into a stockbroker. Doesn't even wear a ball cap any more.

"I tell him I wasn't all that good, and even if I was, that doesn't mean anything as far as his life is concerned."

Ken used to coach when Graham was younger, but now he won't even be an assistant. I know. I asked the night I called to tell him Graham was on my team.

"He puts enough pressure on himself without me being in the same dugout," Ken told me.

We've talked about this before.

Ken tries to diminish his brief baseball career, but Graham won't have any of it.

"He asks if I ever wore a Cubs uniform, and I tell him, well, yes, if you count hand-me-downs. Then he asks if I ever got paid to play and I can't deny that either.

"That closes the book as far as Graham is concerned. I was right up there with the greats of the game and that's all there is to it. What I did as a player is just that much extra baggage for him to carry."

Ken tells me Graham recently copied down all his professional statistics. He keeps the piece of paper by his bed.

"I've told him over and over again that I'd love him just as much if he never gets another hit as long as he lives," Ken goes on. "He looks at me, but the words don't sink in."

The young father stares into the night.

"I used to think getting my picture on a baseball card was the greatest thing that could ever happen. Now I wish it had never been taken."

Mac suggests sneaking the card out of Graham's pocket and putting it where the sun doesn't shine.

Ken smiles.

"Put it this way," he says. "I've been helping people invest their money for 11 years, and I haven't recommended Topps yet."

The driveway is soon cleared, and the kids go home to late suppers. Mac and I retreat to the TV room to plot strategy.

Do we want to let Caleb pitch all six innings and max out for the week, or save some for the second game? Do we want Evan to catch the entire time? Should one of us give K. B. a high-five and get it over with or let nature run its course?

Then it hits us.

These little boys still count "One Mississippi, two Mississippi" when playing hide-and-seek. They still like to climb on the see-saw. They still get wide-mouthed over puppet shows.

"We're grown men," Mac says, "and here we are obsessing over whether our group of fourth-graders can score more runs than their friends."

He flies thousands of miles a year across the country to submit bids on construction projects.

There's plenty to worry about.

What if he puts a little too much padding into his final figure and misses landing an important job by only a few thousand dollars?

What if he cuts it too close? What if his bid is the lowest, but it doesn't give his company an adequate profit margin?

I write five columns a week, and every one is supposed to be interesting.

There's plenty to worry about.

Will the story about the guy going to Cuba in a jet ski be a good piece? Will the old black guy who looked after the old white wino be willing to talk about his friend's death? Will readers care that I just saw my best friend in high school for the first time since graduation?

We agree that baseball and the boys provide a much-needed escape from what we do for a living.

He drives to Cedar Rapids—a six-month project with more than 100 jobs on the line—and asks himself if Walter would hit better with a closed stance.

I stare at another deadline and wonder if Graham could get a few more miles per hour on his fast ball if he came more over the top.

The doorbell rings.

It's Technocoach.

He knows us well. "It's only 9:00 p.m. How come you guys aren't out there practicing?"

"The boys are coming back in thirty minutes," I reply. "Mac got us some night-vision goggles."

Every kids' league needs somebody like Technocoach.

Physics teacher. Unmarried and no prospects. No son on the team. Never played baseball as a child, but now watches it all the time. Would rather be around kids than a conference room full of optics scholars. Will coach the only team in the league that practices more than we do. Found out about my SAT scores and, thoughtfully, never says "quantum" in my presence.

This is his sixth season at this level. Sometimes there are enough dads who want to manage and he becomes an assistant. Other years, the dad pool is leaner and he's asked to take on the top job.

The rest of us played ball when we were young and are athletic enough to give the kids hands-on pointers. We can hit grounders and play long-toss with them. We can pitch batting practice and show our catchers how to block pitches in front of the plate.

Technocoach can't do any of these things. So he buys instructional videos on hitting, fielding, and throwing. The kids have a skull session at his house and then repair to the field.

He also shoots tape of some of the league's better players in action to show his kids the proper technique. I had a couple of good hitters last season, and a Camcorder-carrying Technocoach was a frequent visitor to the backyard net.

He filmed me trying to show my number nine hitter that one does not swing one's twenty-nine-inch bat at the ball as one would a twenty-nine-inch hammer if one hopes to move up to number eight hitter.

I was flattered. Tony Gwynn has his own video, and now me.

Technocoach is up front with his parents about his lack of playing experience. He says the tapes, his enthusiasm, and volunteer help from fathers and big brothers should carry the day. This wouldn't cut it in a more competitive situation. No matter how good the head coach was with the boys, there would be an outcry if he tried to hit fungos to the outfield and the ball got no farther than the pitcher.

I think back to the TV show I saw about the mean-spirited Little League program in Maryland that too often degenerated into shouting and even fighting. The other coaches would laugh Technocoach right out of the park.

But we'll gladly take him.

And, hey, he's getting better. I watched one of his practices last week and he's this close to being able to warm up his pitcher without needing a chest protector.

I notice he's limping.

"Sprained ankle. Hurts like hell." He pulls off his sock. I've never seen blue like this except on the flag.

"You know how long it takes to put the bases in? Well, I thought we could save that ten minutes and go right to catching fly balls. It's not that we don't need the practice.

"So I'm at home plate and walking backwards toward third. We had just missed our fifth ball in a row and I was POed. I'm raising my hands and hollering and reaching in my back pocket for another baseball when I go down like one of those characters in a Mortal Kombat game.

"I stepped in the hole left by the base, and my ankle was laid out like a side of beef. I wanted to throw up and cry at the same time.

"Here's where it gets weird. I goof around with the boys a lot just like you guys. They saw me go down and thought I was pulling some kind of joke—you know, pretending to roll around in the dirt because they were such bad fielders. "I'm dying out there for what seemed like five minutes before my catcher finally runs up to help. Naturally, there wasn't any ice."

"Wasn't any third base, either," Mac says. "You were doomed from the get-go."

"That figures. Well, I'm in agony on the ground, and the boys start milling around with confused looks on their faces."

"Let me guess," I chime in. "You got on one of them for crying over nothing when the ball clipped him on the finger, and now you look like you're writhing over nothing."

"Something like that. I'm wondering who in the world I'm going to get to teach my classes the next day when it hit me."

"What hit you?" Mac says.

"That I'm responsible for twelve boys by myself. I'm about as immobile as you can get and still be breathing, and somehow I have to hold their attention for another hour until their parents come."

"Where was your help?" I ask.

"One was shooting videotape at Conehead's practice, and the other dad was out buying Big League Chew."

"So what did you do?" Mac wants to know.

"Simple. I conducted a lesson in basic science."

"Beside third base?" I ask.

"Exactly. I put them in a circle, and we watched my ankle swell and change color. I explained exactly what was happening and why I was in such pain. They didn't learn anything about baseball, but they became quite conversational in lower-extremity tissue dysfunction."

Let's see one of those Little League coaches in Maryland give an impromptu kinesiology lesson while flat on his back.

I ask about his Diamondbacks.

"We're pretty good in the field and I like my catcher a lot. Hitting? If we could bat off the batting machine at Two-Bit Sports, we'd go undefeated."

Last year, Technocoach tried pitching to his team. He had the control of someone trying to toss a protractor into a windstorm. Batting practice moved inside, where it is likely to remain for all time.

Twice a week, he rents the forty-five-mile-per-hour machine for an hour. This runs him two hundred dollars or more a season. He never asks for reimbursement. "My penance," he explains, "for stepping in the bucket as a coach."

Rain is in the forecast. Better check the backyard.

One kid's sister forgets doll. One kid forgets Swiss Army knife. One kid's father forgets sunglasses.

◆ Garret Mathews

◆ SWING BATTA!

© Gayle Shomer

© Gayle Shomer

◆ *Garret Mathews*

◆ SWING BATTA!

◆ *Garret Mathews*

© Gayle Shomer

♦ SWING BATTA!

◆ Garret Mathews

All photos pages xvi–xvii © MaryAnne Mathews

◆ SWING BATTA!

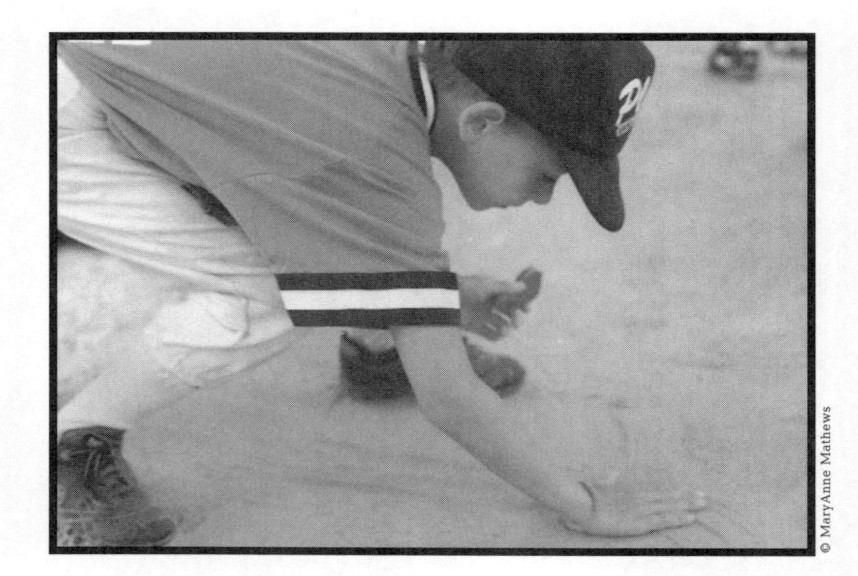

◆ Garret Mathews

◆ SWING BATTA!

7

OPENING DAY—NO PARADE BUT LOTS OF WALKING

Am I nervous about our first game?

Can't spare the time. I'm too busy making sure I haven't forgotten anything.

- ✔ Already-filled-out scorebook to give to official scorer. Much easier to do the night before than while hitting infield.
- ✔ Piece of paper outlining batting order and substitution rotation for players' perusal—printed, not cursive.
- ✔ Strip of adhesive tape to attach said piece of paper to dugout wall.
- ✔ Key for concession stand.
- ✔ Two new baseballs.
- ✔ Reminder note to tell K. B. the game has been blacked out. No TV.
- ✔ Reminder note to suggest to league director that any

concession worker using popcorn popper be asked to sign a waiver.

All the kids arrive on time. They loosen up their arms in the outfield.

My first psychological ploy of the season: I select our five players who catch and throw the best—Caleb, Graham, Vaughn, Evan, and Felix—and position them near where the opposing team is getting ready. The idea is for them to view our glove-popping skill and quake in their size fives.

Mac secretly takes the remaining Cubs to the far side of the fence behind the outdoor toilet. Only those Brewers with binoculars will know that more than half our team stops just short of hollering "Incoming!" when a baseball approaches.

I see a guy I coached with years ago when my son Colin was this age.

Marty is eating a candy bar and trying to fix the popcorn popper. His Phillip is long since out of baseball, but, once a booster-club member, always a booster-club member.

He is semi-retired from the print shop and thus can afford to spend a Saturday morning sticking his hand into salt leavings.

But, back then, he was hustling to keep his company afloat, and, truth be told, probably shouldn't have volunteered to be head coach. He was in the third-base box for most of the games, but I ran the practices and wrote the lineup.

"When's the last time this was cleaned?" Marty says as he removes a gum wrapper.

"Forget the popcorn popper," I tell him. "I do well to keep up with Evan's glove."

"Remember the time we took the kids to St. Louis? Phillip was what, nine?"

Halfway through that season, he got tickets to a Cardinals

game. We left early on a Sunday and got back in time for the kids to at least think about doing their homework. A small support crew of parents led the way, and I joined the players in Marty's van. I remember him talking about maybe having to lay off some employees unless he could land some new clients. Heavy stuff indeed for a typist who has never landed an account his whole life unless you count selling Christmas cards when he was in elementary school.

"That was the time we lost Ned sometime during the third inning," Marty recalls. "Absolutely couldn't find him. Thought we were going to jail for sure."

"Who could forget?" I add. "Then, just when we were about to look up the child-abandonment statute in Missouri, we saw that the people sitting two rows over were paying him to go to the concession stand for them. Ned comes back home with lunch money for two months, and he doesn't have to pay attention when the teacher talks about working on commission."

"Wasn't that the kid who rode to practice on the back of his dad's motorcycle?"

"Same. Had his own helmet. Couldn't understand why he couldn't wear it up to the plate."

Marty holds the popcorn popper up to the light. "Hell, no wonder it won't work. Stupid thing's warped."

He's right. We may have to make a chili cooker out of it.

"Remember when we stopped to eat at the restaurant that puts the jars of hot peppers on the tables?" Marty says. "Never been so sick in my life."

"Hey, you shouldn't make bets like that."

"In the service I used to eat those damn things like Fritos. Thought I could do ten easy. What was I thinking?"

"I don't know, but I'll bet they never used those ashtrays again."

"Remember how the boys laughed themselves silly?" Marty says.

He looks at the field. "God, I miss it."

The kids push and shove at the front of the dugout to get a look at the batting order. There is a chorus of disbelief. Danny second? Is the fix in? What's the payoff?

This is pure hunch. Danny's always been down in the order, sometimes even last. But no kid gets more cranked up to play. And no other kid so measures his worth to the team by his spot in the lineup. If I elevate him in the order, it will be a booster rocket to his confidence, and he might just respond with the batting performance of a lifetime.

"Get one to the outfield," I tell him, "and we'll stop the game."

Mere minutes until we take the field. Time for the speech that will inspire them to win for God and country.

"You or me?" Mac wants to know.

"I did the first one last year and we ended up finishing 4–10. You try."

He gets on one knee and they huddle around.

"Guys, we've worked hard to get to where we are today. Garret and I will be proud of you even if we lose by the Run Rule. But that's not going to happen. Caleb's gonna mow 'em down, we're gonna hit, and we're gonna catch every ball that comes our way. Let's show everybody in the stands how good you are. Everybody get in here and let's put our hands together."

Pause to check for bleeding after an onrushing Evan hits Felix in the back of the head with the catcher's mask.

"Who's gonna lead us out?" Mac says.

I eye-point to Walter.

"OK, today it's gonna be a kid who's playing his first game. Walter, go ahead."

He's momentarily taken aback. Breaking the team huddle is a brand-new concept. But he's not silent long. "C'mon, let's win so they'll give us free Cokes."

"Duh. Both teams get them," Aaron chimes in.

"Winners get bigger cups," says Mac, who can think on his feet quicker than any game-show contestant.

Vaughn at first. Danny at second. Graham at short. Aaron at third. Adam, K. B., and Walter in the outfield.

Felix and Aaron will take turns at third. Walter and Trent will alternate in right field.

Mac warms Caleb up while I tell Felix and Trent to choose another way to decide who sits beside the water cooler other than pushing each other with their butts.

"He's on, Coach," Mac says as their lead-off hitter steps in. "I didn't have to move my glove."

Indeed. Caleb needs just twelve pitches to get the side out in order. The only two nonstrikes bounce off Evan's mitt and sail to the backstop. He's got to get better back there.

We fare no better in our half of the inning. Evan hits one three yards, Danny, two, and Vaughn goes down swinging.

In Minor League, the coach can score even if his players don't.

The third-base box is in enemy territory, mere feet from the other team's fans. Most moms and dads come to the game with their engines in neutral. It's early yet. Some bring cups of coffee; others, the newspaper. Many are yawning. I believe I can play at least a small role in helping preserve this mellowness and even turning it to our advantage.

"Nice play, second base," I holler when their kid throws Danny out.

Never mind that the ball was barely struck and a child of six could have made the play.

I heap false praise every first inning without fail. If nothing obvious happens, I've been known to say kind words about the way their pitcher handles a low return throw from his catcher.

My theory, yet unproven, is that opposing fans naturally assume the third-base coach eats his young. If he rants and raves and stomps his feet, they'll put aside their coffee cups and take the game as seriously as they would a high-stakes sales meeting. But let him spew unsolicited compliments, and they'll conclude he's a decent person, not at all like the thug they had in mind.

The idea is to get them to relax, take it easy, and do what they came to the game for in the first place, which is to ask for tips on refinancing their homes. A passivity is thus generated that I hope will spread from bleachers to dugout.

We begin to take the game over in the second. Caleb throws strikes. Their guy doesn't.

Graham belts one twenty feet, but reaches when the third baseman can't get the ball out of a glove that could swallow a bald eagle. Felix walks. K. B. walks in melodramatic fashion, flipping his bat and slowly removing his batting gloves as he ambles to first. When he finally gets there, he waves to a friend in the stands.

"K. B., the game is this way," I holler. "You're not the official greeter."

First-base coach Mac is more direct. "Knock it off. This ain't no Rotary Club meeting."

Aaron hits a grounder up the middle that plates two runs. Unbelievable.

The last of four horribly wild pitches sails over Walter's head without hitting him. Incredible.

Trent watched Walter play dodgeball from the safety of the on-deck circle. Now it's his turn. He doesn't want to go. We almost have to shove him toward home plate.

"Can't we get the pitcher to back up?" he wants to know.

Trent steps out even before the ball leaves the pitcher's hand. Strike one.

Our number eleven hitter starts to take stock of the situation. The pitcher looks like one of those kids who models sleepwear for Sears. Not what you could call an imposing figure. Not in possession of what you could call a fastball. This time, Trent waits to bail out until the ball is almost there. Strike two.

"Stand in there," I shout.

"We need you on base," Mac calls, more to the matter at hand.

The pitcher goes into his windup, cocks his knee as he would if posing for a jeans ad, and lets fly.

Trent more or less stays put, and hits the ball a distance that makes Graham's boink look like a shot to the gap.

I'd say six feet, but then I don't have Conehead's measuring equipment.

Trent takes off. The catcher collects the ball and almost throws it over the screen down the right field line. Then the first baseman gets in the act and heaves the ball high over the shortstop's head. Trent motors toward third. Now things are getting interesting.

The astonished left fielder stands transfixed, and understandably so. Never has he seen two balls travel so far from their intended targets, and flung by teammates who are good enough that they never have to play the outfield. He kicks it, not once but twice, and then makes the best throw to second base I've seen from that position in six seasons.

Which would be great from the Brewers' standpoint were not Trent rounding third and heading for home. The relay is hopelessly late. Safe! Trent slides, but mostly just for effect.

Home run. If that's not the way you saw it, you obviously don't know how to keep score.

Trent hugs me. He hugs Mac. Through the fence, he hugs his parents.

We increase the lead to 8–1 after four innings, mostly on walks and wild pitches. Evan's not catching all of Caleb's strikes, to say nothing of the pitches out of the zone. But he's hanging in there. One foul ball bounces off an unprotected shoulder caused by a chest protector that sags more than an eighty-five-year-old woman. Another time, he takes one in the wrist when a hitter decides to take an extra quick swipe at the ball after drawing only air the first time. Evan doesn't say anything, but I know my son. After the game he'll milk this into the greatest brush with death since Houdini's water-torture escape.

Mac and I ponder our pitching situation. We play again this week. Should we save Caleb for a couple of innings? Can we assume that surely to goodness the Cubs can get six more outs without our staff ace?

"Let's get this game and worry about the other one later," Mac says. "Bird in hand and all that."

I agree. There's important momentum to be gained by winning opening day. And you never want to lose when one of your guys socks a round-tripper.

We win 10–3. Caleb is masterful in a complete-game performance. Four hits. Two walks. One bruised catcher.

Following a game, the good Minor League coach always finds something positive to say about each player. Sometimes it's a stretch.

"Evan, way to hustle to the backstop after the ball kept getting by you."

"Felix, way to throw the warm-up ball back into the dugout without being told."

"Vaughn, way to compliment Felix for throwing the warm-up ball back into the dugout.

"Walter, way to know how many outs there are.
"Danny, way to give the umpire his drink."

I tell the boys we'll have to pitch someone other than Caleb on Wednesday. I also say we've got to hit better if we're going to beat the better teams.

To drive the point home, I tell them if we had been playing Money Ball out there today, I would have been out only the amount of a Hershey bar.

We put our hands together.

"Go-o-o Cubs."

I suggest we go to McDonald's. We've saved the town's women and children. Time to celebrate.

Danny comes up to me on the way to the car. I've never seen him so serious. "Can I bat second again next time?"

"We won, didn't we? Can't change the lineup after a victory."

He sprints to his mom and dad, hollering louder with each stride. "I'm still batting in the same place as the good players."

They don't understand why he is so happy. They smile and clap politely as they would at the Philharmonic.

The equipment bag is way too light. Must've forgotten something. I turn to go back to the dugout when I see Evan wearing what I should be carrying.

"Don't you want to take off the catcher's gear?" I ask.

"Maybe later."

"But we're going to McDonald's."

"I know."

Then it hits me. Evan wants the dining public to know exactly how he spent his morning. I manage to talk him out of the mask. We're going to eat, I explain, and that's where your mouth is.

But he leaves everything else on, and takes his seat beside team members who await their food in the manner of baby robins. (I deliver following victories.) To make sure everyone in the restaurant sees him, he tramps to the bathroom several times more than necessary.

The real Cubs couldn't eat all these french fries. Evan comes up with an idea. Go to Playland. Pretend game is in extra innings. Give Caleb a handful of fries instead of a ball. Use a Big Mac box for home plate. Evan, with mitt, gives the sign. See if Caleb can throw strikes.

I pretend I don't hear. I'm off duty. And, hey, maybe Evan will learn to look the fries into his glove.

There's a tap on my shoulder.

Trent and his dad. Bad news. Trent is losing too much weight. The doctors want to try a new batch of enzymes. He's got to keep up his strength. Baseball is out.

His parents got the news an hour before the game. Trent already had his uniform on and was throwing his ball against the garage. "This was the first time I haven't done what the doctors told us," Trent's dad says. "He was going to play in this game. I couldn't take that away from him."

Trent is hiding behind his father. He's crying and doesn't want me to see.

I don't know what to say. I've never coached a little boy who has a disease that could kill him before he gets out of high school.

Mac comes up. He overheard.

"We'll be thinking of you, Trent," I stammer awkwardly. "Come back as soon as you can."

Nervous silence.

"Yeah," Mac cracks. "We need you on base."

Everybody breaks up.

And they say all an assistant coach does is coach first.

8
A LIFE'S LESSON FROM THE SNOTTYBUTTS

We start Vaughn against the Dodgers. Bad move. He walks six. They don't hit, but they don't have to.

Second inning. We bring in Graham, and give Caleb a try at catcher. They get three straight dink hits. Frustrated, Graham loads the bases on two walks and a hit batsman. We're down eight to zero, and there are no outs.

I try to settle Graham down. Hey, you're the guy we want out here. Just throw it over the plate and let our defense go to work.

He nods. The next batter hits a grounder to Evan at shortstop that goes between his legs. Graham looks my way as if to say, OK, now we have proof there's a conspiracy. When do we launch the investigation?

Caleb's getting into this catching thing. He calls time and walks to the dugout.

Him: "We need some signals for me and Graham."

Me: "But Graham doesn't have but one pitch."

Him: "Don't matter. I want to signal."

Me, rolling eyes: "Very well. One finger for down the middle. Two fingers for on the corner."

Him, hustling back to his position: "Yes!"

Mac, looking squarely at a loss of major proportion: "You should have given him one more. Three fingers means hold the ball and hope for a thunderstorm."

Graham, who should be completely confused, instead responds with deadly accuracy. Seven pitches. Two strikeouts.

The next kid hits a shot between shortstop and third base. The ball ricochets off Evan's forehead to Aaron at third, who steps on the bag for the forceout.

"I get the assist. I get the assist," Evan says when he gets to the dugout.

We hit like we pitch. When Caleb finally gets one out of the infield, their statue of a right fielder catches it.

Down twelve to one after four, we try Felix. "Pretend you're pitching in the backyard batting net," Mac advises. "Just don't hit the side supports and you'll be just fine."

He walks the first batter on four pitches that aren't even close, but never mind that. This kid fires the ball pretty good. And it's all arm. His legs are just for getting to and from the mound.

"There's your next project, Mr. Pitching Coach," I tell Mac.

Felix manages to get every third Dodger out. This is the best our pitching corps has done all afternoon, so we leave him in the last two innings.

We lose going away. Time for the most demanding public-speaking performance of a lifetime.

Forget speaking before a joint session of Congress. Forget speaking to a group of sixth-grade girls before a Hanson concert. Try addressing your players after losing 15–1 to a team that dropped its opener nineteen to four in a game that was called after three and a half innings so five of the Dodgers could go to the Science Fair.

Me, shuffling feet and making little or no eye contact: "Games like this are going to happen, boys. We're not that bad and they're not that good. We have to put this behind us and look ahead."

Danny, still mad because he struck out twice: "I hope somebody knocks their science experiments to the floor and they don't even get a score."

At this point, the good Minor League coach would reprimand his second baseman for poor sportsmanship. But I see it as a welcome bit of hostility that may have a carryover effect and ignore the remark.

Me: "Sometimes you have a test at school that gets the better of you. Maybe you make a 'C' or even a 'D.' What do you do the next time?"

All the boys, more or less in unison: "Try harder."

Me: "Exactly. Let's look on the bright side today. We might have found us a pitcher in Felix. Caleb looked good behind the plate. Adam didn't strike out. Vaughn, you're certainly throwing hard enough; now you just have to get the ball over the plate. Evan, if you can make an out with your face, think what you could do with your glove.

"It's still early in the season. A lot more games to measure us as a team. You guys hang in there and we'll see what happens."

I wait until the boys leave to ask Mac to grade my speech.

"Decent except for the measuring part. We want them to have their minds on baseball, not filling a beaker up to the top line."

Good point.

I'm almost ready to walk to the car when I spot Conehead in the first-base bleachers. Just the person I want to see. His team lost the previous afternoon and I'm dying to find out how that could happen. Maybe watch him wiggle a little.

"Joey was sick."

Often the best explanations are the simplest ones.

Something is wrong. Conehead isn't wearing his bank visor. He didn't make any scouting report-type entries in the notebook he always carries. And he is strangely quiet.

"I embarrassed Jeff yesterday and it isn't going away."

His son Jeff is the team's second-best player. Joey's absence gave him a chance to shine. Conehead was anxious to see how he'd do.

"Tie game in the fifth and I have him at shortstop. First batter hits an easy grounder. He catches the ball, sets his feet, and almost brains the first-base umpire. Runner on second.

"I hollered at him, but real quick. Just a 'Jeffey, you've got to make that play.' I thought that was just a blip on what, up until then, had been a blank screen. But I saw a panic in his eyes I had never seen before. Joey was gone, and it was like Jeff knew he couldn't pick up the slack.

"Of course you know where the next batter hits the ball. Right at Jeff again. Doesn't have to move an inch. He catches that grounder fifty times in a row when we're practicing. But it bounces off his ankle and goes into center field. Runner scores.

"I forgot all about the little boy who asks Daddy to pour milk on his cereal. I couldn't understand why he was playing like this on what could have been a breakout day for him. This time my reaction was more like, 'JEFF, you had better get yourself in the game.' It was twice as loud as I ever talked to any of the other boys, and my eyes were boring right through him.

"You want to think your son will respond by looking your way and giving an indication that he's going to catch the next one. But that wasn't what happened. Jeff was visibly shaking and his confidence was completely shot. He walked to his left a good fifteen feet until he positioned himself almost directly behind second base. It was like he was saying, 'Now I won't make any more errors because the ball probably won't come my way.'

"I screamed for him to get back to where a shortstop belongs. Sometimes our third baseman and first baseman forget where they are and almost stand on the baseline. I notice, but usually don't say much because I don't consider what they do all that important. But this was my son, and no son of mine was going to hide behind second base."

"Let me guess," I said. "Later in the inning, another batter hit another ball to shortstop."

"A pop-up. Easiest play of the three. It hit the top of Jeff's glove and fell out. I remember thinking, if I had a gun, I would have shot him. He let two runs in and that's what beat us.

"I called time and stormed onto the field. Jeff was terrified like there was this big monster coming toward him. I let him have it one more time as I took him out of shortstop and stuck him in right field. He finished the inning crying with his glove over his face."

"Let me guess something else," I said. "By the end of the inning, you realized you had acted like a complete asshole."

"Didn't take that long. As soon as I got back to the dugout, I knew I had made one of the biggest mistakes of my life. But then something happened that made me feel even worse.

"Their next kid made the third out. It had been a long inning, and our guys should have been happy to finally get to sit down. But they stayed put. There was this wild man on the bench, and they felt safer out in the field. The umpire had to shoo them in."

"So what did you do?"

"Called a team meeting right then and there. I told them I had never been so wrong in my life. I had said wrong things and

I had done wrong things, and there was absolutely no excuse for my behavior. Then my eyes met Jeff's, and it was all I could do to keep from crying. Then I apologized nonstop for the next five minutes."

It takes a few moments for this near-tearful image to set in. Conehead. Major cog at the bank. Major suit and tie. Attends fund-raisers with governors and senators. Almost always wins the league championship because he knows every kid on the East Side and thus drafts better than the other coaches.

"Last night, Jeff watched TV by himself in his room. I knocked on the door, but it was locked. When I called out, he turned up the volume.

"Then this morning he got up thirty minutes early so we wouldn't be in the kitchen at the same time."

He looks down at his feet. "You probably think I was here to scout the Cubs and the Dodgers."

"The thought," I reply, "had occurred to me."

"Nothing like that," he says quietly. "It's because I'm afraid to go home. If Jeff rejects me again tonight, I'm not sure I can take it."

I tell him about the time I shouted at Evan.

"Were you ashamed?" Conehead asks.

"Try mortified."

"You always look so calm when Evan is playing," he says.

"I'm anything but. I want to see him knock the hell out of the ball just as much as the other dads. The difference between us is that I'm more of a realist. You guys have dreams of your sons suiting up in high school and even beyond. I've been around kids' baseball a little longer, and I know how good a player has to be at ten and at twelve to have a decent shot at that level. I don't set my sights, or Evan's, that high. If he makes it that far, it'll be our little miracle.

"The way I look at it, he's doing me a favor simply by playing. He's allowing me to be around both a game and an age level that I love. Sure, I'd like for Evan to hit for the cycle and throw three guys out trying to steal second, but I've been around him enough to know that that's probably not going to happen.

"But it is possible that he can be good enough to want to play next year and maybe the year after that and maybe the year after that. Each season is an added blessing because playing—and practicing—is something we can do together.

"I always watched the World Series alone until last year. I can't tell you how much it meant when Evan came downstairs with a load of popcorn and sat down beside me. It was like when I was a kid and my best friend came over on Saturday afternoon to watch the Yankees on the black-and-white TV. After almost forty years, I have a playmate again. And the best thing about it is he never has to go home."

It feels funny talking like this to Conehead. While we've coached against each other since our sons were in T-ball, the relationship has been limited to me shaking his hand after getting beat and him accusing me of making off with his baseballs. Now all of a sudden he's looking at me as if I wrote all the parenting manuals.

"What do you think I should do?" he wants to know.

"Well, since you asked, I've always thought it's a bit much to have your players do calisthenics in the outfield for fifteen minutes before the game."

"I don't mean about baseball. I mean about Jeff."

"Take him to the go-cart track. After a few hot laps, he'll forget the whole thing."

I'm chuckling. Conehead, he of the five hundred dollar suits and spit-shined Bostonians, has never darkened the doorway of such a non-Standard & Poor's establishment. He sees the grease and oil on the owner's jeans, correctly assumes the guy can't even spell "escrow," and stays away.

"My problem is that I'm too serious around the boys," he says. "I need to be more like you."

"Hey, you kick my ass every year."

"Right now I'd trade ten Ws for Jeff not locking the door on me."

"So you really want to loosen up?"

"Definitely. When Jeff looks at me, all he sees is a six-foot disciplinarian."

I tell him about playing Home Run Derby with the boys at the tennis court. "You have to have dumb-sounding team names or it's no fun. Guess what the kids decided to call themselves?"

Conehead has no idea. His imagination begins and ends with "beneficiary."

"Snottybutts and Navel Lints."

"You're kidding."

"No, and the Snottybutts won in extra innings."

"I don't think I could say that word in public. It just wouldn't want to come out."

"Dignity?"

"Something like that."

I tell him about Krishna, Adam's dad, and his unsuccessful attempts to hit my change-up.

"You mean you wasted practice time on a parent?"

"Sure. It was hysterical. The boys are still laughing about it."

"But you could have worked on throwing and catching. That's what I would have done."

"And we could sure use the work, too. But the boys have to have fun with baseball. If they look forward to coming to the field, they're just naturally going to do better."

"But Navel Lints?"

"Hey, no worse than Devil Rays."

I'm happy to share my romper-room theory of coaching, but it's getting late. "Go home. Jeff will probably be waiting for you."

Conehead trudges to his car like a man who's lost twenty straight.

"Cheer up. You've got the Cubs coming up. That's sure to bring joy to your face."

Faint smile.

"I'll give you two pylons if you don't pitch Joey."

Backward glance only. No sound.

Where's Mac when you need him?

9

WRESTLING OVER A TOUGH LOSS

We trail the Tigers 21–20 going to the bottom of the sixth. The game has lasted just short of forever. Errors. Dog loose in right field. Baby sister loose in left field. Pitching rubber rots completely out. Postponement seems imminent until Mac gets the idea to dig one up from the adjoining field and replant.

And there is something else.

The drum major of a home-plate umpire forgot his face mask.

Determined to avoid dental work, he flinches on every pitch that isn't down the middle. Unwilling to declare a strike on something he doesn't see, the ball calls mount up.

Result: Walks, walks, and more walks.

I catch on to this at the one-hour mark. Hmm, might as well use the umpire's fear of a damaged gum line to our advantage.

Me, with arm around Felix in the batter's box: "I want you to take a strike, OK?"

Felix, nodding his head: "Right."
Walk back to third-base coaching box.
Felix swings as hard as he can at a pitch a foot outside.
Return trip to plate.
Me: "What's the matter? I thought you were going to take a strike."
Felix: "I thought that meant take a strike and hit it as far as I can."
Me: "It means don't swing at any pitch until after you have a strike called on you."
Felix: "Does a foul count?"
Me, exasperated: "There shouldn't be any foul because there shouldn't be any swing."
Felix, puzzled: "Usually I get at least one foul ball."
Umpire: "C'mon, guys, break it up."
Me, whispering: "The pitcher's wild. Take a strike."
Back to coaching box.
Felix swings at a ball well over his head.
Return to plate.
Me, waving hands in demonstrative fashion: "What's going on, Felix?"
Felix: "He didn't call it, so I was going to hit it."
Me: "The umpire couldn't call it a ball because you already made it a strike."
Felix: "Oh. So what do you want me to do now?"
Me: "You've got two strikes. Gotta be swinging."
Return to third-base box.
The next pitch is down the middle. Felix doesn't take the bat off his shoulder. Side retired.

"It's not going to be our day," Mac says, shaking his head. "Fate."

Every kid on the field scores at least once. Home plate, which started the game in little better condition than the pitching rubber, is in danger of being trampled to death.

Evan opens the sixth with a hit. Danny flares one over the first baseman's head. Vaughn socks one to center. Bases loaded. Nobody out. Need one run to tie. My best hitter up. And even better than that, an umpire who won't call a strike unless the delivery is perfect.

The Tigers call time.

I amble over to Mac at first. "Shows what you know about fate," I say.

Mac is still cautious. "Bad things can still happen," he replies. "The game ain't over until the bats are in the bag."

Caleb strikes out. It's his first whiff of the season. Panic begins to set in. If Caleb can go down like this, so can Aaron and K. B..

There is something else.

It's bad enough that the Tigers' hurler has discovered the plate. Now the maskless umpire has suddenly found his nerve. It's as if the drum major is saying, "Marching season is over; teeth be damned."

The count goes to two and two on Graham. I tell Evan to steal home on even the slightest wild pitch.

Ball three is way high. Their catcher doesn't even touch it. The ball sails to the screen. Evan takes off. Because fate sides only with teams whose players know what "Take a strike" means, the ball bounces against the rubber covering that protects the bottom of the screen, caroms straight back and drops into the catcher's mitt like a lollipop from Grandma. Evan is out by ten feet.

Naturally, Graham gets a hit on the next pitch.

Bases loaded again.

K. B. comes up. Confidently eyeing the crowd, he takes his warm-up swings.

I feel good, too. Last night on Sportscenter, Craig Biggio came up in the same two-out situation and hit a liner to left to win the game. The segment was repeated every hour the rest of that night and on into today. I'm sure K. B. saw the high-five part. I only hope he noticed the base knock.

Strike one. The crowd of between thirty and thirty-five is on its feet.

Strike two. The dog that was loose earlier senses the importance of the moment and curbs itself. The baby sister has already done her part by falling asleep.

K. B. nubs one in front of the plate. No way they throw him out at first.

Which, naturally, they don't have to do. There's a force play at home.

The pitcher picks up the ball, loses his balance, and starts tumbling toward the plate. Danny speeds home from third. The game hangs in the balance. Who will arrive first? The player at full throttle or the one on all fours?

The kid puts the ball on home plate an instant before Danny's toe gets there.

Game over.

Bats in the bag.

Stunned, I remain frozen at my third-base post. Never have I lost one like this.

"Blame it on the surveyor," Mac says. "If he'd put third base just five inches closer to home plate . . ."

The second-guessing starts almost immediately.

I should never have sent Evan.

I should have had Caleb crouch down until his strike zone became almost invisible.

I should have made the Tigers fix the pitching rubber.

I should have given Felix a video on how to take a strike.

"When I get frustrated on the job, I pick up something heavy," Mac says. "Here, why don't you put the scoreboard back in the shed? Maybe that'll help."

It doesn't.

I mope over to the bench where Mac has gathered the fate-cursed Cubs for the post-game wrap-up.

You do it, I tell him.

"Boys, we just lost an extremely close game, but things have a way of evening out," Mac intones. "I guarantee we'll win one like this before the season is over. Don't any of you go jumping off any tall buildings."

Everybody laughs except Walter.

"You don't have to worry about me," he says seriously. "I'm afraid of heights."

"Garret and I knew this would be a tough game pitching-wise since we decided to save Caleb for the Orioles later this week," Mac goes on. "It certainly wasn't all bad out there. Danny got one to the outfield, Walter only struck out three times, and Evan and Aaron pitched pretty decently considering they haven't had much practice.

"Let's start thinking right now about the Orioles. They're the only undefeated team. What will that make us if we beat them?"

"Good," Graham concludes.

Mac gives one of the best incredulous looks I've ever seen. "Good? Is that all? If we beat them, we'll be the best in the league. Personally, I can't wait. I know we can do it."

We put our hands together. Team dismissed.

I'm still replaying the game when Walter comes up.

"You said we'd go to McDonald's after the game, remember? I talked to my mom and everything."

The season has been a success even if we don't win another game. Walter's mother trusts me. How much? After a recent practice, she let me use her van when I didn't have enough room for all the boys who wanted to go to Lazer Tag.

I wince. The last place I want to go is McDonald's. One of the customers might have seen the bottom of the sixth inning and want to talk about it.

But if he says I promised, I guess I promised. "OK," I holler, "who wants to get something to eat?"

Five hands go up.

"Pile in, but be careful. Last time somebody knocked out my dome light with his bat."

"It was Vaughn, coach," Mac says. "Only thing he hit all day."

Walter is wearing a New World Order T-shirt under his jersey. Danny notices it, and a wide-ranging discussion of pile-drivers and death grips ensues.

If you've never eaten hamburgers with ten-year-old boys who watched cold-cocking professional wrestling the night before, here's what you've missed:

Danny: "I like Steiner the most. When he puts a Torture Rack on you, it's time to call the doctor."

Evan: "Idiot. Don't you know anything? That's not his signature move. It's the Steiner Recliner."

Graham: "Yeah, Danny. If you don't know, don't talk."

Danny, trying to save face: "OK. I'll bet he uses the Torture Rack to get them ready for the Recliner."

Vaughn: "He can't use the Torture Rack. That belongs to Lex Luger."

Danny: "Duh. So what's gonna happen if Steiner uses it. Is Luger gonna sue him?"

Evan: "Shut up."

Walter, proudly: "In school today I traded action figures of Diamond Dallas Page, Disco Inferno, and Booker T for Goldberg."

Evan: "That Goldberg could kill you."

Vaughn: "If I was wrestling, I'd be the Giant and choke-slam everybody."

Walter: "Bet you couldn't choke-slam Sting. He'd just throw you right off."

Vaughn, defensively: "He'd throw you off, too."

Graham: "I like the one who does the Russian leg sweep. What's his name?"

Other boys in unison: "Raven."

Graham: "Yeah, that's it, Raven. He's ugly, but he's good."

Evan: "Not as good as Goldberg. That guy can kill you."

Vaughn: "One time Wrath almost autographed my arm."

Danny, disbelievingly: "What do you mean almost?"

Vaughn: "My dad got real good tickets, right down front where they make their entrance."

Walter, impressed: "You mean where the girls dance and the smoke comes up?"

Vaughn: "Yeah. Wrath came running out and he was heading right for me. I got my pen out and started waving it."

Walter, breathlessly: "So what happened?"

Vaughn: "Just as Wrath took the top of my pen off, Saturn sneaked up from behind and tried to put the Death Valley Driver on him. The pen went flying."

Danny: "So you didn't get the autograph?"

Me, by way of explanation: "Being pile-drived to death would have a negative effect on one's writing ability."

Vaughn: "They started going at it right in front of us. It was awesome. I could feel their spit."

Danny: "I'll bet they were really being careful around you. If they hurt a little kid, they'd get sued."

Evan: "I wish somebody would sue you. Then you wouldn't talk about it so much."

Walter, confused: "What's a sue?"

Graham: "That's when a judge puts his hammer on the table and takes all your money."

Danny, in the manner of a law-school professor: "That's not a proper definition. When you sue somebody, you're bringing a civil action, usually as a result of a tort of some kind."

Evan: "Shut up."

Danny: "You guys are so dumb you'll probably end up being professional wrestlers."

Vaughn: "It would be worth it if I got to put a Death Valley Driver on you."

Danny: "Shut up."

10
SLIDING PRACTICE WITH A LAKESIDE VIEW

I bring my blind friend Chase to the game. The nine-year-old boy had recently been given a tandem bicycle, and I interviewed him for one of my columns.

That day he showed me his special baseball. You pull the pin and it beeps. He hits by tracking the sound as it approaches the plate. It took me a while, but I finally threw the ball where he could hit it.

"Just a single," he said. "You should see me when I do good."

Chase was born with a potentially fatal optic nerve disease. Both eyes had to be removed when he was only a few months old.

"I went to a St. Louis Cardinals game and saw Mark McGwire hit a home run."

He grinned. "That's not quite right. I heard him hit it. The people went crazy. I could feel the stands shake."

Pause.

"If I caught that ball, I guess I'd be pretty famous."

I asked Chase to describe what he thinks a baseball stadium looks like.

"A big, wide-open field filled with what you call green. There are lots of people sitting in little chairs that go straight up. They eat lots of hotdogs, too."

This gave me an idea. "Would you like to go to another baseball game?" I asked. "A smaller game than the one in St. Louis, but a game just the same?"

His face lit up.

"My youngest son is on a team," I explained. "The head coach isn't much, though. The guy just got through losing 21–20 when his team had the bases loaded and nobody out. But he's a decent individual and he'll let you sit on the bench."

Chase comes early and I walk him around the field. He feels the plate, the bases, and the fence. It wouldn't be a bona fide tour of a kids' ball diamond without including the outdoor toilet, so I have him give that the once-over, too.

"Gross."

I introduce Chase to the team and pronounce him honorary captain.

"We're playing our most important game of the season today," I tell the boys. "They haven't lost and this new kid is gonna spur us to victory."

Mac is pumped. "Win this game, guys, and we're number one. I don't care what the record book says."

"What do we get if we win?" Aaron wants to know.

"We'll do something crazy," I reply.

Privately, it's hard to be optimistic. They have two pitchers who throw harder than Caleb. They also have two guys who can reach the fence—two more than the Plaza Cubs.

Chase whispers in my ear. He wants to say something to the team. "You know, inspirational."

I tell him we can use all the help we can get.

Chase waits until he has everybody's attention. Then he shouts, "Kick some booty."

The boys laugh.

I lead him to the dugout.

"One of the kids in Braille class told me that," he says. "It's not a bad word, is it?"

"If it helps us beat the Orioles," I reply, "we'll sew it on our uniforms."

Evan opens the game by drawing three straight balls. Then he proceeds to strike out. We get runners to second and first but don't score. I tell Evan we need him to start helping us.

We get their lead-off guy out, but the next two batters hit grounders through the infield. Evan blocks three pitches in the dirt, but the next one gets by him. Runners on second and third.

"If we can get out of this inning giving up only two runs, we've got a chance," I tell Mac.

I give the fist sign to Evan. This means Caleb is to throw a change-up.

Their kid is totally fooled and hits a little pop-up toward first.

Evan is also fooled and takes a step toward third. I look at him and then track the ball. I conclude he has no chance to make the catch. But that's OK. Don't touch it, I breathe. Let the ball hit and bounce foul.

But wait.

Mask and all, Evan dives. A cloud of dust erupts that's bigger than he is. Did he or didn't he?

The ump raises his hand. Out! Their lead runner is three-fourths of the way home. He slams it into reverse. Evan gives chase. Aaron is playing third. He won't catch it. Don't throw. Run him down.

The boy is too far ahead. Evan will never catch him in all that gear. Be glad we got one out.

But wait.

The runner slips. Evan falls over him and hits the ground face first. The mask goes one way, the mitt another. Evan's head appears out the side of the oversized chest protector. He has hold of the ball. How, I do not know. The runner doesn't know either and is summarily tagged out. Double play!

"How about giving up no runs?" Mac shouts.

"No-brainer," I bellow. "Means we're going to win."

In the early going, I provide a running commentary for Chase of who's on base and what the score is. But I discover that's not necessary.

"If the other team's doing good, I can tell by the noise on that side of the field," he explains. "If we're doing good, then it's right in front of me."

Walter doesn't pay attention in right field and the warm-up ball hits him in the knee. When the inning is over, he limps into the dugout. Then he sees Chase. Suddenly no more hobbling.

I ask why.

"I just couldn't," he whispers. "That kid's blind. All I got is a little bruise."

Fifth inning. Tie game. Bases loaded. Two outs. Adam up.

Their coach calls time. Time to bring in his best pitcher.

I watch him warm up. No way Adam hits this guy.

"He throws fast, doesn't he?" Adam says from the on-deck circle.

There's no point in denying it.

"I'm not good enough for him yet. The ball's gonna be by me before I can swing."

"Maybe not," I reply, not wanting to give up hope altogether. "You've come a long way since the first practice."

"This is a big time in the game, isn't it?" says Adam, who still isn't keen on everything that's going on.

No point in denying this either.

He sets his jaw.

"I'm gonna let it hit me."

"Might hurt."

"I don't care."

"Tough way to get an RBI."

"What's an RBI?"

I explain.

"Do I have one yet this year?"

"No."

The umpire signals for play to resume.

The first pitch comes in. Adam is right. He swings way late.

The next offering sails inside. Adam doesn't move. Plunk. Right on the arm.

His dad, Krishna, leaps down from the bleachers and presses his face against the fence.

Mac meets Adam halfway and walks him to first.

I ask if he's all right.

Mac whispers to him and then hollers back. "He said, 'Let's play. We're winning.'"

Relieved, Krishna returns to his seat.

I sprint to our dugout. "Did everybody see what Adam did?" I shout. "How can anybody make an out after that?"

They can't.

Evan hits. Danny hits—well, pokes. Vaughn hits. Caleb hits. Graham hits.

We're up 7–1. Three more outs to go.

Adam asks to play third. We tried him once and he dropped an easy pop fly. Since then we've gone with Aaron. But who am I to turn down a kid who just got his first RBI?

Mac looks at Adam's shoulder. It's stiffening, and he can barely lift his arm.

"I don't think he can catch," Mac says.

"Maybe he won't have to," I reply.

Caleb walks the first batter on four pitches, a sure sign he's tired.

I bring in Vaughn, who strikes the next kid out. Then a line shot to center. Then a double past Walter. Suddenly it's seven to three.

We try Graham. He gives up a hit and two more free passes. The go-ahead run is at the plate. Only one out.

I call Evan over to the dugout. "Go talk to Graham. Tell him if we don't get out of this thing pretty soon, I'm going to let Danny call a team meeting on the mound."

Evan relays the message. An ashen look comes over Graham. Anything but that.

He brings two right down the middle. The third misses by less than a seam.

"This is too much for my nervous system," Mac says, after pleading for the call. "I won't be able to go to work tomorrow."

The next kid hits a bullet to first. Vaughn spears the ball just as it goes over the bag. Out! Their runner on third has strayed about fifteen feet off the base. Vaughn throws across the diamond. Hard. Too hard for Adam, our late-inning replacement. I pray this will be the first ball ever fired to third in the history of the game that hits the extreme bottom of the base and locks in place. All our kid must do to record the out is dig the ball out while standing on the sack. No muss, no fuss.

But wait.

Adam is positioning himself for the catch. The throw is high, but not unreasonably so. C'mon, kid, raise that sore right arm just one time. Do this thing, and Mac and I will obtain the best shoulder surgeon money can buy.

The ball hits the heel of Adam's glove. It starts to fly away, but he secures it with his free hand. He holds the ball over his head as if preparing an offering.

We kick booty!

I do a dance with every Cub I can get my hands on. Then some moms, a couple of dads, and even one great-aunt.

Evan, Graham, and Caleb put Adam on their shoulders. They make it halfway around the infield before collapsing in a heap. Mac hoists Adam and takes him the rest of the way.

Tears are pouring down Krishna's face. Adam runs over and jumps in his arms.

We go to the concession stand to get our Cokes. I don't know who threw the first one. Danny, probably. In seconds, it becomes a free-for-all.

Krishna gives the concession worker a ten-dollar bill. "Keep them coming."

The boys aim several dollars' worth of soft drink on Mac and me. Then Krishna. Then more on each other. Then for no reason at all they douse the third-base line.

"I thought we were going to do something crazy if we won," Aaron says.

My eyes are almost sugared shut. "And this isn't?"

Mac takes this as a call to action. He grabs the hose from the shed and drags it behind the dugout fence. "Sliding practice!" he hollers.

A small lake soon forms.

"Line up," Mac says, "and let's get rowdy."

I notice that we don't have a home plate. Can't slide in under an imaginary tag unless there's an imaginary home plate.

Krishna throws down his Coke-coated madras shirt. "No good anyway."

Danny first. He dives head-first and wraps his hand around

what a few moments earlier was a functional piece of menswear. He bounces the last few feet on his butt and almost slides out of the pit. A magnificent performance.

Umpire Mac gives a "Safe" call that can be heard a quarter-mile away.

We alternate umpires. Hose in hand, we alternate grounds crews.

Soon the boys are dripping mud. It's almost impossible to tell the smaller kids apart. On some, the only flash of skin I can see is the half-inch under their eyes.

Grown-ups laugh themselves silly.

Felix's uncle: "I just cleaned out my truck. I hope he has cab fare."

Graham's dad: "They look like the orphans from 'Les Miserables.'"

K. B.'s mother: "They look like the Loch Ness Monster just had babies."

Mac tells everybody to stand clear. He announces we are about to witness the rarest of feats: A dry-land cannonball.

A hush, more or less, falls over the crowd. A forty-year-old man is going to do something really stupid.

Mac runs. He gets airborne. He lands on the small of his back in a foot of ooze.

Unlike Adam, he rubs it. "Now I know I ain't gonna work tomorrow."

I ask Chase if he had a good time.

"Almost."

Huh?

"Is there still some mud left?"

I tell him enough for future generations.

"Well."

Well, what?

"I want to slide, too."

Evan takes his hand and walks him to the morass. "Take ten steps," Evan advises, "and then just let yourself go."

Chase slides home as if he's been doing it all his life.

"Safe!"

My wife, always thinking ahead, passes out trash bags. Poke out holes for arms and legs and insert player. New Wave clothing.

I tell the boys to huddle up.

"You, too, Chase."

Pause for a few seconds while he finds his way.

"OK, let's put our hands together. Today was a tremendous team effort. We might not be able to beat the Orioles ten times in a row, but we sure did do it once. And let's have a big round of applause for our honorary captain. He was our good-luck charm."

The boys make over Chase like so many proud grandmothers. An already big smile becomes new and improved.

I was surreptitious in the second inning; Mac, in the fourth and fifth.

Stolen baseball count—plus three.

11
BRINKSMANSHIP AND THE KID FROM RIGHT FIELD

Earlier in the season, I told the boys everybody would get to pitch.

Today, K. B. Fifteen minutes before the game, I send him down to the practice mound with Mac.

The rest of us go over signs. Then I warn them about a play I saw this coach pull in a game a week ago.

"Runner on second, or a runner on first or second. No outs or one out. On the first pitch, their kid squares around as if to bunt. The baserunner or baserunners advance halfway. If the third baseman runs in to field the bunt, they take the base free of charge. It's the same thing as a sacrifice only they don't have to waste a time at bat.

"What we can do to defense this," I go on, "is have our pitcher field the bunt. The third baseman stays home in case there's a throw. He doesn't charge in. That's important. Everybody got it?"

Solemn nods all around.

Actually, it's not all that important at our level. If a kid gets to second early in an inning, he's probably going to score anyway. An isolated piece of cerebral brilliance isn't going to countermand a bunch of walks and wild pitches. It's more the principle of the thing. In the game I watched, their coach pulled the third-base play in consecutive innings. Both times, he smirked something awful. I'm determined to avoid that.

The umpire hollers for the game to begin. K. B. heads for the mound. I ask Mac how he looked.

"Can't say."

"What?"

"Because I don't know. When we got there, he had to take his jacket off. Then he had to put his shirttail in. Then he had to tie his shoes. This was all done at the speed of the space shuttle being trucked to the launch pad.

"Then he kicked the rubber a few times like he's seen on TV. Then he fooled around with the dirt in front of the mound. Then he did some stretching exercises the way he's seen big-league pitchers do on the warning track before a game."

"So when did he finally get around to throwing?"

"About forty-five seconds ago."

"So how many practice pitches did he get in?"

"Two."

It takes K. B. ten minutes to walk the first two hitters.

I've never seen such gyrations on the mound. The kid's not pitching as much as he's winding and unwinding himself. Hand to belt. Hand to cap. Leg up and then back. Arm back and then over. Head up and then off to the side. In order to make it even more difficult to throw strikes, he strides toward the concession stand.

I run to the mound. "When you take this long, you're wild.

When you take this long, your defense goes to sleep. Unless you hit fast-forward, you're back in the outfield."

I'm close to being mad. It's like he's being a smart aleck without having the ability to back it up. Can't he see this gamesmanship isn't working?

K. B. finally throws a strike and there's a grounder to first. Vaughn fields it about five feet from the line. Plenty of time to step on the bag. He could even fall down and make the play.

But wait.

K. B. is covering first. A bit late, but he's on his horse. Instead of waving him off, Vaughn decides it's a shame to have his pitcher run that far for nothing. So he patiently holds the ball and waits for K. B. to get parallel to first base the way Roger Clemens would if he were in town. Vaughn makes a perfect flip. K. B. catches it and steps on the bag just like they do at Yankee Stadium.

Perfect, except the runner beats the throw by ten feet. We should have had an out. Instead, we share our toys.

Line drive to right field. Felix does a nice job of keeping it in front of him. Their kid takes a wide turn at first.

But wait.

Felix holds the ball. Their kid goes a little farther, just to see how well the Cubs secure their borders. Still no throw. He takes off for second. Felix finally airs the ball out. To first.

Naturally, it's over Vaughn's head. The runner proceeds to third. Vaughn can't find the ball. Evan runs over to see if he can help. He's retrieved many balls he launched into our woods and assumes this experience will come in handy. Their runner, seeing that no Cub is within forty feet of the plate, strolls home.

I have a chat with Felix.

"Never throw behind the runner. Ground ball to you, hit the cutoff man or throw directly to second if you think there's going to be a play. A right fielder throwing to first is a no-no. Got it?"

He nods.

I have a chat with Evan.

"You can't be like a stray dog behind the plate and just wander off. The next time there's a lost ball, sit tight for at least ten minutes. If we haven't found it by then, we'll call you in on the case."

We make a couple more horrible plays. It's 6–0 before we finally get them out.

Naturally, we go down one-two-three in our half of the first.

"We need a spark, coach," Mac says. "Here's why you get paid the big bucks."

I call a team meeting. "Remember how well we played the last game? That's how badly we're playing today. We can still turn it around, but we've got to start right now."

Aaron, who missed an easy grounder, goes into give-up mode. "We don't have a chance. We might as well quit now."

Mac spirits him away, and with a flourish. They have a talk.

"We seem to play better when it's Caleb's turn to pitch," I continue. "We field better. We hit better. We even think better. Tell the truth. How many of you guys think the only chance we have to win is when Caleb's on the mound?"

A show of hands indicates an overwhelming majority.

Not having a clipboard, I throw the catcher's mitt down on the dugout floor. "You've got to stop believing that. It doesn't matter who's pitching. What does matter is how we play behind him."

The boys are locked on my every word. I should have been a motivational speaker.

"I'm going to prove to you that I'm right."

I toss the ball to Danny. "Get 'em out."

The boys are flabbergasted. Danny? He's the only kid on the team who didn't get his heater measured by the radar ball because he couldn't throw the minimum speed necessary for the gizmo to work.

"Yeah," I say, knowing what they're thinking. "Danny."

Mac waits until we hit the field, then asks if I've lost my mind. A gerbil, he says, wouldn't be afraid to bat off Danny.

"Just my point. They have the lower end of the order up. The ball will look like a big fruitcake coming in. They'll be so eager to hit that they'll swing at anything."

"Might work," Mac concedes.

"There's something else, too. Whatever else you say about him, Danny's a competitor. We'll get everything he's got."

He tries to walk the first hitter, but the kid will have none of it. Danny throws one high and two feet inside. Foul down third. Danny's next pitch misses the outside corner by an equal distance. The kid steps on the plate and lofts a foul by first. Vaughn catches it against the screen. One out.

The next batter hits a screamer to the right side. Graham, our fill-in second baseman, jumps and catches it. Nothing against our new hurler, but had Danny been in that position the best he could have done would be to offer an early-warning signal to Felix in right.

Unlike K. B., Danny has a quick windup. The waiting comes after the pitch. I swear I could type my name and address in the time it takes the ball to reach its destination.

Their hitter ducks down. The ball hits his bat. Strike one.

On the next pitch, the kid backpedals two steps in the batter's box as he waits for the ball to come down. When he swings, the bat almost knocks Evan's mask off. The umpire rules offensive interference. I've never seen that called, and I'm not even sure the proper penalty was meted out, but who am I to argue with an appliance salesman of an umpire? Strike two.

After checking his face for missing parts, Evan sets up outside.

Way outside. Danny puts it more or less on target. Later, Evan would tell me in all seriousness he wanted his hurler to waste one.

The next offering is top-of-the-cap high. Their kid gives it a woodchopper special. Strike three!

Danny walks off the mound like he's been doing this his entire career. The rest of us know better and mob him.

I tell the boys we don't want to wear Danny out. Too much of a good thing and all that. Graham will pitch the third.

The Cubs begin to climb back in the game. Two runners on. Vaughn creams one to left center. K. B. gets his first decent hit of the year—a bouncer up the middle that gets by their center fielder.

Fourth inning. Down three.

Their lead-off guy doubles. Time for the bunt. Time to go into the prevent-smirk defense.

We're one good play away from regaining the momentum. Forget what I said earlier. Maybe we can get it right here. I flash a palm-down signal to Evan which he relays to Caleb at shortstop. Caleb touches his cap, his way of telling us he's in on the plot.

Pitchout. Evan throws to Caleb.

There's no bunt. Two seconds later, there's no runner either. Caleb tags the unsuspecting fellow out before he can get back to second.

I'm going to demand a raise.

We go ahead in the fifth. Walter and Aaron walk at the bottom of the order. Vaughn, Caleb, Graham, and Adam deliver consecutive hits.

Graham turns his ankle on second base. It isn't serious, but he shouldn't pitch.

Up two runs, I call on Evan. A definite Coach-Daddy here. I

want to see if he has enough poise to close out the game. He strikes the first guy out, but the next kid triples over Walter's head in left. Then a roller back to the mound. The run scores, but we get the out.

Their number three hitter fouls off four pitches before drawing the walk.

I hang my head. The next guy is three-for-three.

One pitch later, it looks like he's going to be four-for-four. A one-bounce line shot to Felix in right. Their kid enjoys his handiwork and lopes down the baseline.

But wait.

Felix comes up throwing.

To second, as he's been instructed?

Of course not. He guns it to first.

And is the throw high or off-line or bouncing crazily? I mean, this is what you'd expect.

No, it's perfect.

And is Vaughn even on the base to receive the ball? I mean, it's certainly not in his job description to accept an assignment from the outfield.

No, he's standing right there.

Out by an eyelash.

Cubs win.

I sprint to right field. "Felix, that was the play of the year. Under no circumstances are you to pay attention to anything I tell you for the rest of the season."

Mac pushes Aaron front and center. He announces our third baseman/left fielder/emergency pitcher has something to say to the team.

Sniffing, Aaron stares at the ground. "I'm sorry I said we weren't going to win. I was mad because I didn't do good."

Mac wants to know if he's learned his lesson.

"Yes. I don't want to have to make another speech."

Danny's parents didn't get to the game until late. They missed seeing him pitch. But they're hearing about it now.

"The key to the game?" Danny says, asking himself the question. "Had to be the slider I started working on last week. They absolutely could not hit that pitch."

Danny demonstrates the proper grip and then has his father try it out.

"No, what you've got is more of a slurve," Danny says, suddenly an expert on the subject. "Here, move your thumb and forefinger over."

His dad does what he's told, but the ball keeps falling out of his hand. "Gee, I don't see how you throw a ball like this."

Danny shrugs his shoulders. "Get in a big game like this, Dad, and the adrenaline takes over."

I stuff the equipment in the bag. This is sweet. I actually feel like a manager. If I pushed any more buttons out there today, I'd be a seamstress.

Danny runs up to me. "Thanks."

"You're welcome, but what for?"

"Just thanks."

A strap on the face mask came loose. It will be Mac's homework assignment. But the repair job will have to wait until after our coaches' meeting.

"Halfway through the season," Mac points out. "Gotta evaluate our personnel."

We sit on the back porch. Gentle breeze. Six-pack at our fingers. Snack bowl filled with boiled peanuts Mac brought up from Alabama. Beagle pups at our feet. Baseball count at plus five.

A perfect night. Nothing could make it better.

"Yeah," Mac says, "who needs a meteor shower when you've got a two-game winning streak?"

We issue our own scouting report.

Evan is improving behind the plate and is becoming more accurate with his throws. The problem is that he hesitates. We need to teach him to throw as he comes out of the crouch. Needs to hit better in the clutch. Tough to strike out, but sometimes is satisfied if he just puts the ball in play. I can always tell if he has a good at-bat by how vocal he is the next inning behind the plate. After a recent double, he kept a running commentary with the hitters that went something like this:

Evan: "I'd be a little afraid to bat right now if I was you. Vaughn's a wild man out there. Almost knocked a kid's eyeball out last game. Rescue Squad had to come."

Batter: "Liar."

Evan: "No, serious. Took two doctors and a nurse to push it back in. Blood was all over the place."

Batter: "Liar."

Evan: "If you don't believe me, ask Vaughn. He got a souvenir eyebrow."

Batter: "Mister ump, make him stop."

Umpire: "No way, son. I usually have to work a high school game to hear stuff like this."

Danny is hanging on to his number two spot, but barely. He needs to make more contact.

The news is better on the scientific front, though. Danny has dissected two baseballs and a broken fungo bat. After the season, he wants a crack at the chest protector.

Both of us noticed that Vaughn almost got excited today when Danny retired the side in order.

"It was like he started to run up to Danny and give him a good shaking," Mac says, "but then thought better of it and went to sit by himself on the bench."

I mention the rip-roaring Mac who orchestrated the impromptu sliding practice and did the cannonball.

"Definitely not a like-father, like-son," Mac admits.

"Vaughn laughed at you, though. I saw him."

"Sure, he did. Went home and told his mother all about it. He got a big kick out of the fact that his daddy was right in the middle of the mud pile, but he was strictly an observer."

Maybe he'll go to work for the United Nations, I point out. They've got lots of guys like that.

Mac brings K. B.'s name up, which results in much head-shaking. Neither of us has been able to get him on track, and we're fast running out of patience.

Skill-wise, Graham's our second-best player, and he's a hard worker, never missing a practice. But he heaps pressure on himself to live up to his father.

It shows up the most at the plate. He tightens up instead of letting his natural ability take over. The smooths he displays in the field become awkward stutter-steps in the batter's box.

"We talked about it last week at the backyard net," I say. "I asked him what he thinks about when he's hitting. He said he imagines how his dad would murder the ball and then he tries to do the same thing."

Aaron. Another tough case.

"We had our little talk today," Mac says, "but I don't think that's the end of it. If something doesn't go his way, he has a hard time dealing with it. Boom, his mouth starts going."

I tell him about the trailer park.

"His background is so different from the other boys," Mac replies. "Probably has a lot to do with it."

"Yeah," I add. "We forget how good we have it sometimes."

Mac gives me a get-well card to sign for Trent. "Guess who bought the card and passed it around in the dugout?"

"Danny."

"How did you know?"

I tell him about Danny thanking me for letting him pitch. If a kid is that thoughtful after the excitement of a game, just think how he is if he has an opportunity to think about it.

We go back over Felix's play in right field.

"You think we were dying in that 21–20 game," Mac says. "Look at that poor guy in the other dugout today. Game's on the line and he can't get his best player to first after the kid smoked it to the outfield. Tell the truth. Did you think Felix was actually trying to throw him out?"

Some things you don't share with anybody, not even your assistant. "Let's just say it was good coaching."

Walter has been every bit the project we predicted. The sum total of his offense so far has been two foul balls. On every ball hit to him in the field, he's either missed it, kicked it, or held it forever. As far as baserunning is concerned, his best play has been advancing on a walk.

"But I've never seen him less than one hundred percent happy," Mac says.

"Think he'll ever get a hit?"

"First off, the ball would need to be larger, at least the size of a soccer ball."

"He squints a lot, too. Could be his day vision isn't too good."

"Maybe put a tracer round in the ball."

"Couldn't hurt."

"Nice boy, though. When he sits beside me at McDonald's, I almost want to take him home."

Adam. Two thumbs up. By far our most improved player. Started the year batting last. Could move up to fifth or even third.

Caleb has been awesome. He's hitting at least two line drives a game, and he's by far our best pitcher and shortstop. Give him a few innings back there and he'd be our best catcher.

Mac turns serious.

"You heard about Caleb's dad?"

For a second I can't place the guy. Then it hits me. The screamer. Big guy. Construction-worker type. Got in an argument with Caleb's coach in the seven-year-old league and they almost got into a fight. Nasty divorce. Ended up moving to Florida with his girlfriend.

"He's coming in pretty soon to watch Caleb play. They say he's even worse than he was three years ago. Word's out he carries a gun."

That's just great. Not one incident with a parent all season and now this.

"There's something else," Mac goes on. "Maybe I shouldn't tell you this, but they say he's mad about us having sliding practice. Said Caleb could have hurt himself and got knocked out of all-stars."

I can't believe this.

"Just goes to prove there's a lot of sorry-ass people in the world," Mac says, shaking his head.

"You're the one he ought to be going after," I say accusingly. "You're the guy who got the hose out."

"Hey, I'm just the assistant, old buddy. But don't worry. I'll stand behind you all the way."

Behind me. Yeah, right.

"I think I'm being pretty brave. Bullets have been known to go through people."

12
CONNECTING WITH YOUR SON ON JUST PENNIES A DAY

I can think of only one time in four seasons that I've beaten Conehead.

It was last year, and I had big-time help from the umpires.

Church field. Bases loaded. His clean-up hitter drives one way over my left fielder's head. The ball lands on the parking lot, takes two bounces, and rolls under the Sunday School van. You could take up the collection in the time it takes us to retrieve it.

But wait.

The bowling ball salesman of a home-plate umpire applies the seldom-used asphalt rule and declares it an automatic double. Two runs score instead of four.

The high school junior of a base umpire was my oldest son's teammate in the pitching-machine league. The kid almost never brought money to the field, and there's no telling how many hamburgers he hit me up for. He'd always promise to remember next time.

Last inning. Two outs. Conehead has the tying run on first. The kid tries to steal second. Our catcher's throw is high. The runner slides under the tag.

But wait.

The base ump calls him out. We win. It was like after eight years he finally remembered to pay me back.

I get to the field about thirty minutes before the game. Conehead pulls in right behind me. He's usually at least an hour early. I ask if a bank meeting ran overtime.

He shakes his head. "I've changed some things around. A half hour's plenty."

I notice something else. None of his kids are here. He always requires the bottom of his order to report for extra batting practice.

"Cut back on that, too."

His players straggle in. They report to the dugout, not to the outfield for stretching exercises.

"I figure they're loose enough after a day in school. I know I would be."

Could my eyes be playing tricks? Is one of his boys playing a hand-held video game beside the bat rack?

"Guess he wants to sharpen his reflexes before the game," Conehead replies, shrugging his shoulders.

This is a new Conehead. Relaxed. Soft-spoken. Less authoritarian. The old version would have exploded if a player had a video game within a thousand feet of the on-deck circle.

I apply one final test to find out if we are indeed dealing with a changed man.

I bring up last year's game; the mere mention has always made him turn crimson. "Remember the base umpire when we beat you guys? I ran into him yesterday at the mall. You'll never guess what he wants to study at school."

The guy I used to know would have grunted, "Remedial umpiring."

This new version politely asks about the young man's parents and says, "Anthropology? Well, isn't that great. Fine choice. Nice fellow."

My players know the routine by now. When they get to the field, they are to put their batbags and water bottles behind the dugout bench. They will then pair up in the outfield. Short tosses until they warm up, and then heaves of an approximate distance from second base to home. They are to throw to each other's chests. Obviously, this rarely happens or the Cubs would have a better record. To prevent arguments, I instituted another rule: Forget the party of the first part. Players are to take turns going after errant balls. Unless there's an emergency along the line of getting hit in the cookies, they are not to bother me until I've finished visiting with the opposing coach.

I remember how down Conehead was the last time I saw him. He had hollered at his son during a game and was heartbroken about it.

I ask about that while we put the bases down.

"We're back to normal. Praise be for Penny Toss."

I don't follow.

"It's something we did as kids. My brother and I would roll down the car windows and throw coins at road signs. We nailed the stop sign at the end of the street so many times the highway department finally had to replace it."

"You dog," I say. "So you actually did something wrong growing up."

"Hell, yes, and that's the thing I started thinking about with Jeff. To him, I'm somebody who went straight to adulthood without ever being a kid. He sees me as somebody who's always in a suit and always deadly serious.

"I told myself, OK, if I can introduce the governor at a campaign rally, I can figure out a way to get on the same wavelength with my son.

"A couple of days after the big blow-up, I took him for a ride, just the two of us. This was different than any ride we had ever taken together. I didn't talk about his next game or getting better grades or anything like that.

"I gave him a pile of pennies and kept a handful for myself. We're going down the road and here's this school-crossing sign coming up. I lean out the window, draw a bead on it and, pop, dead center, just like I used to do. You could hear the pop in the next block.

"Jeff dropped his jaw. He had never seen me do anything remotely like that.

"Go ahead, I told him. Gauge the speed of the car and remember to let go early.

"At first, he was timid. He'd throw, but then he'd duck down so nobody could see him. I said, 'Hey, don't worry. I'll take the rap.' That did wonders for his aim, and pretty soon he was bouncing them off the guardrail.

"Then we graduated to miles-per-hour signs. I'll bet I went up and down the same stretch of highway ten times. He'd hit the target and then I'd try to match him. We're laughing and joking with each other. It was great. I didn't know I could be like that. By the time we got back home, he forgot all about what an idiot I'd been."

I bring up the kid who's playing the video game in the dugout.

"After that bad time with Jeff, I rethought the way I do things. I realized how many rules and procedures I had established with a bunch of ten-year-old boys. Everything had to be exactly by the book. I was like the principal at school that everybody's afraid of.

"Well, that's over with. I told my team we're still going to try to win and we're still going to have respect for coaches and other players, but I'm no longer going to be the troll under the bridge. No more screaming. No more finger-pointing. I'm going to relax and enjoy myself."

We shake hands and wish each other good luck.

"You pitching Caleb?" he wants to know.

I'm surprised he even asks. Despite this sudden transformation, he remains the coach I most want to beat.

"By the way, you heard about his dad coming up from Florida?"

I repeat what Mac told me about the gun and the guy being pissed off at me.

"Better watch your back. I know the man. He's one mean hombre. If he says he's going to do something, you can bet on it."

Mac hears the last part of the conversation. "Hey, you in the crosshairs," he wants to know. "Got our starting lineup? Everybody's waiting."

My pre-game pep talk is decidedly low-key. There are no secrets about Joey. Last year, he played on an AAU team that went to the national semifinals. In his last start, he pitched a no-hitter and struck out seventeen.

"The true test of any sport is how you do against the best." I point to Joey. "He's the best. Let's make it a challenge to see how well we respond."

Mac whispers, "We're gonna get challenged clean out of the park."

Caleb pitches manfully, but Joey alone is almost enough to give them a five to zero lead. Going into the last inning, we've put the ball in play only four times. They obliged with a couple of fielding miscues, but we still don't have a runner past second.

Caleb's up for the third time. Joey tries to put a little extra on one, but misses low and inside. Caleb's rope-jumping act is too slow. The ball hits him in the lower leg. He's down like a shot.

Caleb tries to be brave, but the tears flow. An ugly knot forms almost immediately. Just to be on the safe side, we decide to take our injured player to the emergency room. Mac carries our fallen hurler to his mother's car. He'll follow in his truck.

A somber Conehead offers to take Joey out. "Your kids were scared before. Now they're probably terrified. Whatever you think."

It's a tough call, but I take the position that we've got to learn to get through this.

And, to a lesser degree, so does Joey.

I shake my head, and the game goes on.

As I suspected, Joey has enough control to work the outside part of the plate. He gets our next three guys out without coming anywhere near inside.

After the game, Joey asks me where they took Caleb. He wants to go see him. Conehead does, too.

I think back to that win-or-else Little League in Maryland. We should make a videotape of what Joey and Conehead just did and mail it to them.

The game ends thirty minutes early. Walter's mother hasn't picked him up. We sit in the bleachers and wait.

Me: "Are you glad you're playing baseball?"

Walter, beaming: "Yeah. Now I want to be on more teams."

Me: "This is your first one?"

Walter: "Unless you want to count safety patrol."

Me: "How come you never signed up?"

Walter: "I used to bring the papers home all the time, but my mom never would turn them in. She thought I'd embarrel myself."

Me: "You mean embarrass?"

Walter: "Yeah, so then I just started leaving the papers in my locker."

Me: "Well, I'm glad she changed her mind."

Walter: "She might change it back. I'm almost on probation."

Me, astonished that my number nine hitter could be in stir: "What?"

Walter: "Not the police probation. The Mom kind. I used to be in the dumb school until this year and then I got transferred to the smart school and then—"

Me, interrupting: "There is no such thing as the dumb school."

Walter: "I made good grades there, but it's a lot harder where Danny and Evan go. Mom doesn't want me to be embarreled. She says one more 'F' and I'm gone."

He unzips his batbag and takes out a folded sheet of paper.

Walter, proudly: "Social studies test. Look at the grade. Best I've ever got."

It's a 'B+.' The teacher has circled it and added three smiley faces.

Me: "Congratulations."

Walter: "You know why? It was that blind kid you brought to the game."

Me: "Chase?"

Walter: "Yeah, he can't even tell what's on his test paper and he does all right. At least I can see it. I ought to do good, too."

His mother shuts the car door and starts to cross the street.

Walter runs up to her. "Mom, Mom, I almost hit another foul ball."

She smiles and tells him to wait in the front seat.

"Thanks for staying with him," she says. "The twins had a soccer game and I'm running late."

I tell her about seeing the social studies paper and all the smiley faces.

"He's worked so hard since changing schools. It's really a

struggle for him. When something good happens, you want to celebrate."

She looks uncomfortable. "I haven't always done right with Walter. He got laughed at a lot early in school, and that made me real defensive about letting him do things. I felt like if I kept him with me nothing bad would happen. He'd bring the sports sign-up sheets home, and I'd make up some kind of excuse why he couldn't play.

"He kept hounding me about wanting to be on a team, so I finally gave in this spring. He's been so happy playing ball. It's really been good for him. I wish I hadn't been so afraid all those years."

I ask about putting him on probation.

"Did you ever say something and wish you could take it back two seconds later?"

"Many times," I reply. Without naming names, I tell her about Conehead and Jeff.

"We've got some nosy neighbors, and they knew all about what school Walter used to go to. The word gets put out that your son is slow. People don't say anything, but you see them look at him like there's something wrong. It just makes you boil up inside.

"I guess you could call it selfish of me, but I pushed hard to get him transferred. The new principal said we could try, but he wasn't making any promises. This whole year has been very stressful for both of us. I know I've been guilty of pushing him to stay with the so-called normal kids.

"One night about a week ago I snapped. My job and the running the kids everywhere and the helping Walter with his homework. It all just got to me.

"He showed me an 'F' on a math paper and I lost it. I knew I could get his attention with the baseball team because he's so fond of it. So I threatened to take that thing away from him if he got another bad grade.

"His face dropped. He looked at me like all the pushing I had done before was OK, but now I had gone too far. I knew I had said the wrong thing, but I didn't back down because it would make me look weak. If you're a single mom, you learn that. So I didn't say anything else and neither did he. That's where it stands. Only the worst mother in the world would take the baseball away from him, but I don't know how to undo what I've done."

"Maybe he won't get any more bad grades," I suggest.

She grins. "Maybe your Cubs will win the rest of your games."

"This might sound nuts," I tell her, "but there's this one boy on the team who's extremely smart. Maybe Danny could work with Walter."

"You mean the little boy who plays second base who can't throw the ball very well and runs like there's something stuck between his legs?"

"Yeah, that's the one."

"How bright is he?"

Lady, he could tutor me.

"Well, if he doesn't mind."

Mind? He's waited all his life for a chance to be a visiting scholar.

Mac drives up at his usual sixty miles per hour.

"Caleb's fine. Just a bone bruise."

Macabre grin. "Bet you're relieved, what with his dad coming and all. If he's gonna pull a pistol on you over sliding practice, then what's a trip to the emergency room worth? I'm thinking at least a tommy gun."

"Your concern for my well-being," I say, "is touching."

"Hey, got a few days yet. Still time for disarmament talks."

13
GETTING HURT BY A FOURTH-GRADER

Terry plays third base on a minor-league baseball team based in Evansville. We met one day after practice, and he agreed to keep a diary for their first road trip. I turned it into a couple of columns.

He penned a wonderful account of surviving on $12.50-per-day meal money, practicing bunt defense on the motel parking lot, and waiting three hot hours by the side of the road until the team bus was fixed.

The boys followed Terry's story in the newspaper and wanted to meet him.

"Would you?" I asked.

"Sure."

"One more favor. They want to tell their friends they hit off a pro. Would you throw batting practice before one of our games?"

"Sure."

Saturday morning. I'm not expecting Terry to come. His team

has dropped its first seven games. He could be excused for staying out late Friday night trying to forget.

But he's right on time, and the boys flock to his side. He shows them the proper way to grip the bat and to turn on the pitch as if their foot is trying to squish a bug.

Then it's time to hit.

Evan insists we bat the regular lineup, which makes it his turn first.

The mound is forty-five feet from the plate. I usually pitch from the full distance, as it's safer back there. As an additional protective measure, I also pitch fairly hard.

Because Terry wants to examine their hitting technique, he stands only about thirty feet away. Because he doesn't realize that a ten-year-old will occasionally knock the crap out of the ball, he lobs it in à la Danny.

Evan fouls a couple and then sends a line drive back up the middle. Thud! Right off Terry's right eyebrow. Blood flies everywhere. The substitute batting practice pitcher goes down on one knee. I fetch a cold compress.

"The guys on the team aren't going to believe this," Terry moans. "Getting hurt by a fourth-grader."

I'm no doctor, but I know when a guy needs stitches.

"You owe me big-time," Evan chortles in my direction. "You said we get five bucks if we hit one hard enough to send the pitcher to the hospital."

"What can I say?" I tell Terry. I thought never in a million years.

He arches the eyebrow that still works. "It's getting worse. Fourth-grader collects bounty."

Team members are supposed to report any injury. Terry searches his billfold for the telephone number of the trainer. He bleeds on his Social Security card.

Not wanting the same fate for his truck phone, Mac dials the number and holds the receiver against Terry's ear.

The trainer picks up.

"Uh, you're not going to believe this, but . . ."

The medical man advises the third baseman to sit tight. Help is on the way.

"This is the first time I've ever played baseball and needed a cut man," Terry says.

The boys show their disappointment. Now they'll have to bat off me.

Terry notices a roll of duct tape in the concession stand. He gives me the compress.

"Here, fix me."

I don't follow.

"Tape this over my eye. I'll throw to the others."

I do my best, but within minutes the pitcher's mound looks like the scene of a knife fight.

He finishes pitching to the remaining nine players without incident save a feigned heart attack when Vaughn hits a soft liner up the middle.

The trainer confirms the need for an emergency room. Still dripping, Terry departs the mound.

"Your grounds crew is going to wonder about this," he says.

"Simple," Mac replies. "Pitching coach conducts pagan ritual to pray for shutout."

The glow from batting off a one-eyed professional ballplayer lasts only until the visitors' half of the first. Two on. One out. Caleb at the plate. Huge potential for big inning.

But what's this?

Caleb backs out on every pitch. He takes two strikes and then swings wildly at a ball that bounces in front of the plate. He runs back to the dugout as if glad the ordeal is over.

Graham grounds out and we don't score.

This is the stuff of catastrophe. Mac and I converge on Caleb as one. What's the matter? Did somebody die? Is your mom losing the house? C'mon, what gives?

"I'm scared."

The story comes out in dribs and drabs. The previous game. Joey. Hit in leg. Pain. Hospital.

"I see the pitcher winding up and I think it's gonna happen again."

"You have to have confidence in your ability to get out of the way," I tell him.

"Last time I didn't."

Mac asks how many times he's been hit by a pitch in his career.

"Twice."

"That's not so many," I reply.

"But this one still hurts."

The priest of an umpire tells us we will have to delve into Caleb's psyche at a later date. For right now, he says, you owe me one shortstop.

Third inning. Runner on third. Two out. Caleb gives a repeat performance, backing out even more.

Fifth inning. Bases loaded. Caleb takes a called strike with a full count.

It gets worse.

Easy pop fly to K. B. in center. All he has to do is stand still and open his glove. But he gives the play one of those Ricky Henderson numbers. Eyes darting. Arms flapping. Feet pumping.

And drops it.

He looks at his glove as if to assign blame. By the time he finally gets around to picking the ball up, their guy is standing on second base.

"No excuse!" I scream. "Awful! Just awful!"

Which prompts a warning from Mac.

"Simmer down, bud."

I try, but it isn't easy. It's almost as if the boy is deliberately trying to make me mad.

Naturally, they set our last nine batters down in order. We lose 12–1.

I know K. B. less than any other boy on the team. He's come to most of the practices, but leaves before we go get something to eat. Never engages in glove-slinging. After games heads straight for his dad's car.

He's fine until we get the bats and balls out. Bright, friendly, joking with the other boys. But when the game starts, his TV monitor glows bright red.

We have a talk.

I apologize for losing my temper. I should never holler like that, I tell him, unless you're in the process of robbing a bank.

He's looking squarely at his shoes. This isn't going to be easy.

I ask if he understands why I raised my voice.

He nods, but I explain anyway.

"It wasn't because you missed the ball. That's going to happen. It was because of the way you went about missing it. You looked like the world's biggest show-off."

"I don't mean to."

"You've done it all season," I go on. "Tell me why."

He shrugs his shoulders.

"That's not going to get it done, K. B.," I say, trying to be patient. "It's time to tell."

"But it's hard."

"Do your best."

"To cover up not being very good."

The words are barely coming out. I almost have to stop breathing to hear.

"Last year I tried to catch every ball, but it didn't work. The coach could see I wasn't good enough to play the infield and I never did.

"I watch TV a lot. I know what you're supposed to look like when you do it right. So this year I wanted to make it look like I could catch good."

"So you could play the infield?" I ask.

"Yeah."

I'm beginning to come around. K. B. has zero confidence in his ability, but he tries to hide it by acting like his blustering sports heroes on television.

Up until the moment he drops the fly ball, or lets the grounder go between his legs, the idea is to look like a mega-star so the coach will think he knows what he's doing and that he just messed up somehow.

Giving and receiving high-fives hammers that point home. Players who engage in such behavior must be good, right?

Taking so long to throw is consistent with everything else. If he winds up normally, he believes his assumed inability will become all too obvious. But if he invents a peculiar motion, the coach might focus on that and overlook shortcomings in speed and accuracy.

"Tell me if I've got this straight, K. B. You're very concerned about how you rank compared with the other boys on the team. You believe it's very low. But you believe you can make it higher by pretending to be somebody you see on TV."

He nods.

I tell him I would much prefer the K. B. of last year, the K. B. who didn't put on an act.

"Can I set in the infield sometime?"

"If you'll stop what you're doing and just play."

He looks at me for the first time.

"OK."

We shake on it.

The next game has started. I see Al in the bleachers. Loud. Brash. Works you over like a press agent. You don't want him to buttonhole you on a good day. You sure don't want it to happen after a loss and a talk.

I creep around the concession stand. The guy is leading the cheers. Maybe he won't see me.

No such luck. "Hey, Garret," he shouts, "Come over here and take a load off."

I trudge over.

"Hey, great column in the paper today," he says, pumping my hand.

I didn't have one.

"You seen Darion play yet this year?"

I wince. There's no denying his son is an excellent player. I just get tired of hearing about it.

"No, how's he doing?"

"Burning up the league. Hell, he's batting .800. Probably a record."

"You keeping his stats?"

"Gives me something to do while the other boys on his team are striking out. I'm not doing his slugging percentage this season, though. I'm not into all that higher math."

Darion is batting. On the second pitch, he sends a drive over the center fielder's head that hits at the base of the fence.

"Damn," Al says, throwing his pencil down. "That's fourteen straight at-bats without a home run. This ain't the time to go into a slump."

Evan can't even draw a picture of hitting one that far.

"What do you think Darion's doing wrong? His wrists? Footwork? Maybe the boy needs a new bat."

He's already got four, including one that cost two hundred dollars.

I have to shake my head. No way can a lowly Minor League coach give meaningful advice to such a prodigious talent.

"But look on the bright side," Al says. "Now he's up to .812. But enough about my boy. How's Evan doing? I heard he took one in the face."

"Yes. He was playing shortstop at the time, and alertly turned what could have been a sloppy error into a spectacular assist."

I hate myself when I do this, but a father has to fight back the best way he can.

"Must've been a helluva play."

"Best I've seen at that position in at least two seasons," I reply. "Ball's hit to Evan's right. Runner on second's off like a shot. Evan starts to field the ball, but sees the kid closing in on third. No time to catch and throw. The only way to get the out is to try for a forehead deflection. Evan puts his face at the perfect angle. The ball caroms to my third baseman just ahead of the slide. You can't draw up something like that. The kid just has to have a feel for it."

"Sure saves wear and tear on the old arm," Al says.

"Put a steel plate in Evan's head," I go on, "and he might be able to get guys out at first."

If I'm going to hate myself, I might as well really hate myself.

Graham's dad says he thinks he's figured out a way to solve his son's hero worship once and for all.

"Old movies," Ken tells me after the game. "Come on over."

The projector is in the living room. A dusty stack of Super 8s is on the coffee table. Ken is at the controls. Graham and I take seats.

"Found these in the attic over the weekend," Ken says. "I thought they had been thrown away."

The grainy images are of the same serious young man whose face is on Graham's baseball card.

"Mom came up one weekend when I was in the minors," Ken explains. "She brought the camera and I don't know how many reels of film. She'd shoot until it clicked and then she'd put another one in. You'd have to know her. We had a doubleheader and she shot every second of me hitting, in the on-deck circle thinking about hitting, and in the dugout thinking about going to the on-deck circle."

Ken is batting in the first inning. Not wanting to miss a moment, she keeps him in the viewfinder while she scrambles closer to the field.

"It looks like she was filming while doing jumping-jacks," Graham observes.

Three quick strikes. The last swing was particularly dreadful.

"Slider," Ken remembers.

You can measure his mom's disappointment by the sudden jerk of the camera and a momentary loss of focus.

"Nothing for one," Ken says.

The home movie continues with a side view of Ken in the dugout tapping his bat on the concrete floor. Still tapping, he advances to the on-deck circle. Then to the plate for five last taps before getting into his stance. Four pitches. Three strikes. Only once did Ken offer.

"Nothing for two."

The next at-bat is little better. Ken hits a slow roller to first that is handled with ease.

"Nothing for three," he says, catching Graham's eye.

Now I understand what Ken is doing. He tried telling Graham he wasn't all that good. Now he's showing him.

Ken hits a solid grounder, but slips coming out of the box and is thrown out by a step.

"See, Graham, your dumb old dad couldn't even stand up."

After two more strikeouts, Ken finally gets one out of the infield—a little blooper past third.

The projectionist gives himself a round of derisive applause. "What a mammoth blow that was. Sign that guy up."

The doubleheader ends with Ken striking out on a three-and-two pitch.

"One for nine, and I left the winning runs on base in the last inning," he tells Graham. "Does that sound like some kind of all-star player?"

Graham has to shake his head.

"Guess what happened a week later?" Ken asks.

Graham has no idea.

"I got released. Skipper called me in the office, passed out the money I had coming, and said it was nice knowing me. I was back home in time to take Mom's film to the drugstore."

He looks at Graham. "See, I was just another ballplayer. Thousands of guys were better than me. Take me off that pedestal and put somebody on it who deserves to be there."

Graham runs downstairs. The wrestling is on. "It's Steiner versus Luger, Dad. You coming?"

"Give me just a minute."

I have seen a truly rare thing. A dad who tears himself down to build his son up.

"Level with me, Ken," I say. "These aren't the only films of you playing pro ball, right? Just the absolute worst ones."

He grins.

"Can't talk now. Might miss a body-slam."

14

YEP, IT'S A VISIT FROM THE GIANT

The good Minor League coach never tells himself a game is in the bag. Too many goofy things can happen.

That said, this game is in the bag. Here's why I know. Technocoach is in the opposing dugout.

Felix gets the start. We've worked on his change-up, but I tell Evan not to call any. Off-speed stuff does these last-place guys a favor.

"Just sling it in there as hard as you can," I tell Felix as he takes the mound.

He proceeds to drill the lead-off batter in the back. Which—assuming you're a cold, unfeeling Minor League coach—is not the worst thing that could happen when you're playing a not-very-good team.

Latent fear hastens to the surface and gets right in the bloodstream. Their next three guys offer only token resistance. Even the clean-up hitter looks afraid.

This one, Mac says, is over.

Evan lashes a double to left. I flash the steal sign. Let's find out if their third baseman is going to be a green light or a stop sign.

Their catcher makes a perfect throw, but the third-sacker does a Walter of a catch. Evan scores easily.

Danny beats out a grounder to short and scores on a booming double by Vaughn.

Caleb's up. I had forgotten about his new-found fear, but his first swing reminds me. He steps out as the pitcher delivers, and steps back in only when he sees the ball isn't coming inside. Waiting to swing until the ball is almost past him, the best he can do is send a weak roller to first.

Graham hits. Adam hits. Aaron hits.

The rout is on.

Buoyed by his two-bagger, Evan talks to their already fearful batters about how Felix enjoys hitting people and how much it hurts to have facial reconstruction surgery.

Caleb starts something new at shortstop. Instead of chattering the usual drivel, he boils the verbiage down to a hearty, "Yep." For generations, baseball has been searching for a fresh banality players can holler to assure the coach they're paying attention. This could be it. Within seconds, the entire team picks up on the chant. "Yep" in the infield, "yep" in the outfield, "yep" from the grown men in the Cubs' dugout.

Revolutionary. I get dibs on the marketing rights.

Top of the fourth. Bases loaded. Walter up. He hits a roller to second, his first fair ball of the season. Their kid boots it and then throws wildly to first. Two runs score. K. B. stops at third.

Danny immediately calls time. He walks over to the official scorer and says something to him. Then he heads my way.

"My turn," Danny says.

I'm confused, as any third-base coach would be if a player replaces him during an inning.

"Look at the score," Danny goes on. "You promised."

Now it hits me. Earlier in the year, I said he could coach third if we got up by fifteen runs.

"But you're batting pretty soon. You can't coach and hit at the same time."

"Replaced myself," Danny replies.

I take my seat on the bench. This should be interesting.

Danny starts flashing one sign after another. I have no idea what he's signaling. Aaron doesn't either. He and his new third-base coach have a talk.

Aaron starts to bunt, then pulls back at the last instant and tries to hit. Because many college players would have difficulty doing this, he fails to execute.

"Aw, Aaron," Danny hollers in an annoyed voice. Danny is deadly serious. He called a play that he saw on ESPN the night before and, by God, he expects his ten-year-old hitter to carry out the assignment.

New and different signs are flashed. "You're supposed to tip your helmet if you understand," Danny calls out.

We have just lost any element of surprise, but procedure must be followed.

K. B. breaks for home. Aaron squares around to bunt. Squeeze play! Aaron must get the bat on the ball or our runner has no chance. Coach Danny has reached deep in his playbook for this one.

The pitch is at ankle level and sinking fast. We have trouble bunting strikes, let alone bouncy balls.

But wait.

Aaron chip-shots the thing a few feet in front of the plate. K. B. scores. Aaron beats the rap at first.

Evan is up. He looks at his third-base coach and sees signage normally associated with a tie game in the ninth inning of the World Series.

They confer. Danny is in a superior position and relishes every moment.

"I've never done this before," Evan whispers after breaking the huddle. "I'm not even sure I can."

"Make the play," his coach growls.

Aaron breaks for second. The ball is thrown six inches outside. Evan lunges like a fencer and sends the ball gently to the right side. Hit-and-run! Evan is an easy out, but Aaron rounds second and slides in at third ahead of the throw.

Cubs' parents applaud our best baserunning play of the season, but Danny remains stoic. Like any veteran coach, he put his players in a position to be successful and they simply did what they were told. Why all the excitement?

They finally get us out, but there's fresh buzzing in the dugout. Evan has checked with the scorekeeper. The Diamondbacks have yet to get a hit, and time dictates this will be the last inning.

"Felix has a no-hitter," Evan whispers as he puts his shin guards on. "Pass the word."

Evan's turn to be deadly serious. He calls a meeting at the plate. "Just get close to the ball, guys. Make it look good and they'll rule it an error."

The first two hitters strike out. Then a doink of a pop-up toward the dugout. Vaughn squeezes it as he bangs into the fence. No-hitter!

Evan throws off his mask and runs out to embrace Felix. Caleb and Danny join in. Our three smallest players try to lift him on their shoulders, but Felix is too much for them.

But wait.

Who's that coming up from behind? Why, it's Vaughn—our widest body. Pumping his fist, he puts a bear hug on our history-making pitcher. Bellowing a hearty "Aarugh," he then flips Felix into the sawdust pile in back of third. Then he carries him around the bases and dumps him in front of the concession stand.

I turn to Mac. This is the moment he's been waiting for. Dreamed of, even. Vaughn getting excited. Vaughn showing his emotions. Vaughn feeling a part of something.

We watch the boys drinking their Cokes. Somebody trips somebody and soon they're all rolling on the ground. Vaughn is in the middle of it.

Mac says nothing. He just watches and occasionally dabs an eye.

I ease away. This is his moment. Let him enjoy it.

Technocoach helps me pick up the bases. "You guys have a good team. Other than Joey, that's about the best pitching we've seen."

I apologize for the sideshow in the last inning. "We weren't trying to run up the score," I say. "It was just a case of Danny being Danny."

"Don't worry about it. They were just having fun, and we've been getting hammered like this all year."

"You came out of the draft with less talent than the rest of us," I go on. "The league director should have done something. Maybe moved a few players around."

Technocoach shakes his head. "On the contrary. I'd call it a very good year. Not in terms of victories, because there's only been one. But you wouldn't believe how many of my players are interested in science and the NASA program. I've talked with some parents, and I might take as many as four boys to Space Camp next month."

Mac barks orders on the other side of the field.

"McDonald's. Everybody in the truck. No exceptions. Load 'em up, head 'em out."

He packs three in his cab. The other seven squeeze in the back beside the toolboxes and circuit breaker boxes. Danny and Walter sit together. They review the multiplication tables.

I have to drop the cashbox off, so I'm a few minutes late. When I get there, Conehead and Mac are sitting at a front table with a man I don't know. Big guy. Construction-type shirt. Arms that look like mine supports.

"We want you to meet somebody who's come all the way up from Florida," Conehead says.

Oh, shit, it's Caleb's dad.

There's a formal introduction, but I don't hear the words. I'm too busy staring at the muscle mass. This man is built like a steam engine. He could toss me into the french fryer and not even need his pectorals.

God, why did I let Caleb slide? Why did I let him get hit with the pitch? Why do I practice gun control?

He stands up. At least six feet, six inches tall, and a scar under his eye. He reaches in his pockets. Oh, my God, he's making his play. All I can pull out is a lineup card.

"Glad to meet you," he says quietly. "Could I interest you in one of these?"

It's a religious tract.

"Pentecostal," the man says. "The way of the Lord."

Mac and Conehead break out laughing. To the degree that Pentecostals find humor in mortal fear, the giant offers a small smile.

"Thank you for being Caleb's coach. If you don't mind, I'd like to go sit with him."

Two thoughts race across my brain: I won't be going into the french fryer and Mac and Conehead could teach conspiracy theory to the CIA.

"Har, har, har, we really had you going," Mac says, slapping his side.

"If he'd come one week later, we would've had you so worked up you'd be taking self-defense classes," Conehead adds between belly laughs.

Now they can tell the truth. The big guy found the Lord about two months ago. Stopped losing his temper. Told his girlfriend to move out. Started leading his Local in church attendance.

"He never did pack a piece, though," Mac says. "We sorta made that up."

Conehead heard about the giant's conversion from a secretary at the bank who knows the family. Just a few weeks ago Caleb's mother was terrified of him. Now she's answering his letters.

"The reason he came back wasn't to beat the hell out of you," Conehead says. "It was to try to get back with his wife and son."

"Let me guess," I say, turning to my assistant coach. "You found out about all this and saw an excellent opportunity to scare the crap out of me."

"You got it," Mac says. "Things were going just a little too smooth in our dugout. Thought I'd add a little sudden death to the mix."

A crowd has gathered around Evan. Players, some dads, even a restaurant employee.

Caleb holds a cup. He is part carnival barker, part front man. "You wanna see a show? We got a show for you. Only a quarter. One thin quarter to see the boy make his stomach disappear. Come one, come all. Pay right here. Make the cup talk."

Evan weighs only sixty pounds. Because of the gymnastics,

most of that is muscle. He can take a deep breath and suck his stomach in to the point he pretty much doesn't have one any more. You pay to stare at the gap. It's gross, but, hey, contortionists have a right to make a living, too.

I've seen the performance, so he doesn't get any of my money.

But Mac tosses fifty cents into the cup. "That's for doing it while drinking a soda."

"I can't believe you guys," Walter's mother says, looking at Mac and me and shaking her head. But she's laughing.

Walter is standing beside Danny. Two children couldn't be more different. But that's not important right now. They're on a team, and they're as one watching Evan do something really stupid.

"This has been the best time of Walter's life," his mother whispers.

"Mine, too," I reply.

"Is Walter still on probation?" I ask.

"Yes, but I don't want him to be. I'm trying to think of a way to get around it."

"Call me some night," I reply. "I might have something for you."

Caleb and Evan divide their profits from the impromptu matinee engagement. Two bucks each. Pretty good for not buying print or TV.

Stolen baseball count: plus seven.

15

WHOO, WHOO, A BIG RUN

The last hour of school today is the fourth-grade talent show.

Which explains my presence in the Not-So-Green Room backstage waiting for a ten-year-old girl to finish tap-dancing.

Evan announced the day before his intention to be in the production. Which prompted the following family discussion:

Mother, to Evan: "You are absolutely, positively not going to do that awful thing with your stomach."

Mother, quickly, to father: "And you have no right of appeal."

Evan: "It wouldn't work anyway. The kids in the back couldn't see."

Mother: "Thank God."

Father: "So what are you going to do for talent? It's not like you're an ace musician."

Mother: "He could recite 'Old Ironsides.' The military is in this year."

Evan: "I ain't gonna do no poem."

Father: "Well, what, then?"

Evan: "Spectacular Catch. You and me. I already told the teacher."

Father: "What, we're going to the field?"

Evan: "The auditorium, same place as the other acts."

Father: "I'm not understanding."

Evan: "Simple. You bring a mattress from home and put it on the stage. I'll have my glove. You throw the ball and I'll dive to get it. Just like we do after practice."

Because the mattress wouldn't fit in his backpack, I also had to function as property master. Dragging the thing down the hall, it had to look like I was making a major withdrawal from the nurse's station.

The tap dancer curtsies and takes her leave.

Our turn.

Evan goes to extreme stage right. I stand on the floor in front of the first row of kids.

He gives the signal and sprints toward me. Because I have never played Spectacular Catch under bright lights and in front of 120 people, several of whom are grown-ups, my initial throw is the worst in the history of the game. Very low and very away. Ken Griffey, Jr., couldn't have come up with it.

Evan flashes a look of severe displeasure. I promise to do better.

He re-signals and cranks up his engine.

Not wanting to make the same mistake, I lead him too much. He flops off the mattress, belly-skids on the floor, and hits his head on the piano.

Thunderous applause. Pain knocks 'em dead every time.

After feeling for blood and finding none, he shoots me another dirty look. This time, I insist, I'll get it right.

The sprint. The float through the air. The diving catch. Perfect!

He does four encore presentations, each to diminishing applause.

"Why don't you hurt yourself again?" one boy calls out. "That was better."

His teacher struggles for just the right thing to say. Finally, "Uh, Evan, that certainly was different."

A girl in the front row offers her assessment.

"Dumb, but pretty good."

• • •

Mac is out of town on business. Before leaving, he recruited Adam's dad to be assistant coach. The guy never stops joking.

Krishna insists on meeting me at the field a few minutes early to go over the first-base coach's duties. I have the following anxious conversation with the fill-in:

Krishna: "So where do I stand?"

Me: "Inside the chalk."

Krishna: "Anywhere?"

Me: "Anywhere."

Krishna: "Should I yell something to the batter? I've never done this before. Is one thing to say better than another thing?"

Me: "They're all equally worthless. 'You can do it' works. So does 'It just takes one to hit.'"

Krishna: "What about when somebody gets to first base? What do I do then?"

Me: "First, congratulate him for getting that far. Then tell him how many outs there are. You can also remind him to run on a ground ball and only go partway on a pop-up."

Krishna: "Talk or whisper?"

Me: "Whisper. It's on a strict need-to-know basis. Their first baseman is not on the list."

Krishna: "I think I can remember that. Anything else?"

Me: "Not unless you want to try to make off with a couple of their baseballs. We're up seven, you know."

Krishna: "Should I talk with the other coach? If he says something to me, what should I say?"

Me: "I'd go with 'Fine, and yourself?'"

Just as I feared, the hitters are catching up with Caleb. They know by now that the ball is going to be around the plate. Even though he has better than average speed, they trust him not to be wild. Boys he would have struck out earlier in the season are making contact. The better hitters have gone from weak grounders to hitting line drives.

We're down 8–3 after three innings. Caleb has walked only one, but they've hit six balls hard.

With runners at second and third, Evan pops out to end the inning. It's a familiar pattern. He does a pretty good job of starting rallies and extending rallies, but he hasn't come up with the big hit when we need it.

Caleb insists his arm is sore. His pride has taken a pounding with the eight runs. I suspect he's inventing a malady to explain away his performance. He gets a bag of ice and puts on a pitiful look, but I still don't believe him.

I try Vaughn. He throws his hardest of the season, but control remains a problem. He walks the bases loaded. Graham gets the second out but gives up two hits in the process. Danny lets a grounder go between his legs and we're down ten.

Fly ball to left. All K. B. has to do is take a couple of steps in and it's an easy play. Misjudging the distance, he comes in six steps. He doesn't adjust in time, and the ball falls just out of reach.

But wait.

K. B.'s not doing the TV thing. He immediately goes after the ball, notices the kid trying to stretch the hit into a double, and fires to second. Easy out.

"See what you can do when you just play?" I holler.

Are the Cubs hopelessly down in the score? Yes. But is this going to be a total loss? No.

Adam comes up in the fifth with one out and Graham on first. Krishna is absorbed with his instructional whispering, and doesn't immediately see that his son has absolutely crushed the baseball down the left field line. It lands in fair territory and then bounds in foul ground beyond the fence. It's by far our best hit of the season.

Krishna looks up to see their left fielder on the dead run. He is startled and excited at the same time. He emits a loud "Whoo, whoo" and then starts jumping up and down.

Then I see something I have never seen on a baseball field.

Adam rounds the bag and charges toward second. Krishna is right behind, gesturing wildly and urging him on. "Go, go. Faster, faster. Make a big run."

Never has a first-base coach been so dedicated to duty. Krishna almost steps on second before he realizes what he's doing. So what we have is a little boy going full speed for third, and a sheepish father sneaking back to first and hoping the umpire doesn't see him.

The ball goes under the outdoor toilet. Lost ball in high weeds. Home run!

Krishna runs to the dugout and puts his arm around his son. Somebody should have taken a picture.

Every kid on the team has pitched except Walter.

So Walter it is.

I walk to the mound and show him how to wind up. Evan reminds him to keep his right foot on the rubber.

Krishna comes up to me in a panic. "Walter can't pitch yet. You've got to do something."

I don't follow.

"His mother's not here to see it. She's still at the twins' soccer game. I can go get her, but it'll take a while. You've got to stall for time."

I have Danny change positions with Evan. I also have Danny pretend he has no idea how to put the catcher's gear on.

The two umpires visit the concession stand. Several boys on the other team start building a fort out of bats and helmets. A full five minutes elapses before Danny finally takes his position.

Still no mom.

Walter's first four pitches miss both the strike zone and the catcher, prompting the following exchange with our new backstop:

Me: "The ball's going right by you. Quit closing your eyes."

Danny: "They're not closed. It's just long blinks."

The next kid hits one in front of the plate. Danny is on it with surprising dispatch. With his arm, the distance to second base is a journey across the sands of time. He throws anyway. By the time the ball arrives, the runner has had time to plan his weekend.

Movement behind the right field fence. It's Krishna and Walter's mother at full trot.

"Hi, Mom," Walter shouts. "I'm pitching!"

Is he ever!

Their overeager clean-up hitter almost steps on the plate to send the first pitch high in the air to Graham at first. One out.

Sharp grounder to the right side. Graham dives and misses. Evan makes the play at second, but Graham is over too far to get back to his base. Evan sprints and arrives just ahead of the runner. The resulting collision is the best of the season—hat, helmet, glove in all directions.

After a walk, the next guy slams a drive to center. Oh, no, this inning will never end.

But wait.

I put Caleb out there, frozen arm and all. He tracks the ball as it leaves the bat, our only player with this natural-born knack. Legs churning, he makes a beautiful over-the-shoulder catch at the edge of what would be the warning track if the league had that kind of money.

Walter's mother starts a standing ovation that quickly spreads to our other parents.

"How much for the ball?" she wants to know.

I flip it to her, a luxury the Cubs can afford because Mac and I have been so vigilant all season at finding a home for baseballs that haven't been tied down.

Walter: "I got the save! I got the save!"

Felix: "No, you didn't. We have to win for that to happen."

Me: "Shut up."

Aaron tells me he doesn't have a ride home.

He was one of our few bright lights today, catching a line drive at third and driving home two runs with a pair of hits. I congratulate him on his good game as he gets in the car.

"Mom and Dad are splitting up."

There's no shock in his voice. No disappointment. The words come out in the manner of a radio reporter reading the five o'clock news.

"Me-Maw is going to take the three kids, at least for a while."

I don't know what to say.

"She's done it before," he goes on, shrugging his shoulders. "One time I didn't stay with my mom for baseball and basketball season."

I met the grandmother a few weeks ago. She told me this is her daughter's third husband. "He's the best of the bunch," she said that day at the field. "How would you say it, going one for three?"

Both divorces, the widow explained, sent her daughter into a deep funk. That's when she'd make the phone call. "It was always something like, 'Mom, I need a little break from the kids. Can you help me?' I've gotten to where I can almost tell which day the phone's going to ring."

Once, the time Aaron described, his mom went almost a year before asking for the children back. The other time, the separation was three months.

"It's not like she's a bad parent," the grandmother explained. "She sees the kids several times a week and always does something special on their birthdays. She just can't handle them day in and day out when she's feeling bad like this."

The grandmother assigned no blame and cheerfully accepted the extra round of child-rearing. "I love my baby," she said that afternoon, speaking of her daughter. "If she needs me, I'm here for her."

Aaron takes out some baseball cards from his back pocket. Trying to make conversation, I ask if there are any real Cubs in the stack. He's busy reading the statistics on the back and doesn't hear.

"My first dad gave me these. I liked him the best of all."

The trailer park comes into view. I start to turn.

Aaron shakes his head. "We moved. The last dad couldn't pay the rent." Again, no emotion. Just fact.

He leads me to another mobile home park about a mile away. It's even more depressing than his former neighborhood. Some of the trailers are boarded up. One has burned almost to the ground. Children are throwing rocks at the little that remains.

"See this place?" Aaron says, pointing to an only slightly

more habitable dwelling. "Last month, somebody got shot and they sent the police cars out."

He has me stop four doors down outside a small trailer with fractured awning. Spray-painted graffiti covers the propane tank. An old Chevrolet is on cinderblocks. Two people are arguing inside.

"My mother can't get along with this dad either," Aaron says. "Thanks for the ride. Maybe we'll win next time."

Oh, the game.

I had forgotten.

16

THE ROAD TO THE TOURNAMENT DOESN'T GO THROUGH HAWAII

As usual, Danny is at the field when I arrive. With no one to warm up with, he throws his ball off the side of the concession stand. If it were Joey, I'd stop him immediately, not wanting to see chunks taken out of the cinderblock. With Danny, structural damage is only in his dreams.

I've put off having this discussion for too long. Today is the day, by God. If it makes me the villain, so be it. String me up at high noon. The Plaza Cubs simply can't afford to have Danny bat in the number two hole any more. I know he's going to be disappointed, but we're just not getting the necessary production from that spot in the lineup.

Danny's moving down. That's all there is to it. The good coach can't let sentiment affect what's best for the team.

At least that's what I told myself last night as I rehearsed looking into this little boy's eyes and breaking his heart.

I call him into the dugout. He could make this a lot easier on me by loafing, but naturally he hustles. "Uh, Danny, I've been thinking, uh, ah, er, the tournament is coming up after this game and, well . . ."

"Did Walter tell you about his English paper?" he says. "I helped him with some of the words and the teacher gave him an 'A minus.' That's OK, but we'll get an 'A' next time. Any other boys you want me to make smarter?"

"Uh, no, Danny. Thank you very much. There is, uh, er, this one thing I want to go over with you. It's about the batting order and, uh, er . . ."

"I want to tell you something, too. My family's going to Hawaii next week when we're in the tournament."

"That's exciting, Danny. I've always wanted to visit there. I'm glad you're getting the chance."

"But I'm not going."

"What?"

"I'd rather play ball. I'm going to stay with my uncle."

"But you may never have another opportunity to go to Hawaii."

"Our team is gonna do good in the tournament this year. We might get a trophy. I don't want to miss it." He looks up at me and slaps his glove. "Was there something you wanted to tell me?"

Sue me, but there is no way I can move him down. Let Joe Torre come and do it. "Uh, just this. When you're batting second today, stand a little closer to the plate. Might help you see the ball better."

Caleb gives us two strong innings. We're up three when the rain comes.

Weatherman Mac insists it's just a brief shower and that we'll be able to get the game in.

If you weren't in our dugout during the delay, here's what you missed:

Felix: "How come we don't have a domed stadium?"

Walter: "Because there isn't enough space to park all the cars."

Mac, looking at all the league-furnished equipment: "Garret, remember when we were kids and we played on our own without a bunch of adults to organize things?"

Me: "Sure do. We had our own vacant lot of a field a few blocks from my house. Every kid had a different job to make it playable. Somebody would borrow his dad's lawn mower to trim the infield. Somebody else would steal the flour to do the baselines. Somebody else would steal a section of inner tube that we'd beat in the ground for the pitching rubber."

Mac: "No more. A lot of these boys are better than I ever was, but the only time they play is when some adult rings the bell and says it's time."

Me: "I know. Back then we'd get on the phone and call all the boys in the neighborhood. Game starts at ten o'clock, be there. That kind of thing. Sometimes we'd get as many as ten kids. One or two would have a ball and one or two would have a bat. That's all we needed."

Caleb, puzzled: "What about umps?"

Me: "We called the game ourselves."

Adam, equally confused: "What about fans?"

Mac: "We rooted for ourselves."

Walter, in utter disbelief: "How did you know who won without a scoreboard?"

Me: "A game would last all week with players changing sides every day. Part of the fun of playing was arguing about who was ahead."

Mac: "No video games. No arcades. Only three channels on the TV and none that a kid would want to watch. Might as well play ball."

Me, in total agreement: "There wasn't any air-conditioning back then either. Inside the house was just as hot as outside. Might as well play ball."

Mac asks if any kid on the team has ever gotten on the phone with his friends and organized a pickup game of anything. Baseball, basketball, football—it doesn't matter.

No hands go up.

Me, shaking head: "We had ourselves a time. You boys don't know what you're missing."

Mac, looking at the adult-typed schedule of games and practices posted on the side of the dugout: "If it were any more structured, it could be put in a rocket at Cape Canaveral and launched."

The rain has all but ended. Dads rake the field. Moms towel off the bleachers. The college student of a home-plate umpire checks his watch and worries that he'll be late for the Saturday-night kegger.

Top of the fourth. Tie game. K. B. on third. Full count on Evan. He swings at a ball over his head and grounds weakly to second. Side retired. So what else is new?

Top of the fifth. Still tied. Bases loaded. Two out. Caleb up. He's slipped to seventh in the order. If anything, he's even more frightened than he was the game after Joey hit him. Stands a mile from the plate and steps back even more as the ball is pitched.

Mac and I have tried everything. We've joked with him about getting plunked. We've assured him that only a small percentage of pitched balls in our league are inside because subconsciously most hurlers have no stomach for whacking people. In batting practice, we've put the equipment bag on the third-base side of Caleb's front shoe. Touch the bag, we tell him, and that means you're stepping out. After five minutes, the bag has so many footprints it looks like it's been to a dance.

The futility continues. He waves at three pitches on the outside part of the plate.

We don't score in our half of the sixth. They get the winning run to second off Felix, but he fans the next two batters. Extra innings.

Because Evan is starting things off and not closing things out, he hits a solid single to center.

Danny rolls to shortstop. Their kid hesitates, and Evan slides into second ahead of the force. Adam grounds out, but both runners advance.

Vaughn guides one through the infield, and Evan and Danny race home. Graham and Aaron fail to hit, but we're up two going to the bottom of the seventh.

Can we hold the lead?

No.

Two strikes on their lead-off guy. Felix throws one a little inside that I swear made no contact with flesh.

But wait.

Their kid grabs his arm and jumps up and down as if he's been torpedoed.

I stake my claim of avoidance to the home-plate umpire, who is just about to agree with me when the attorney of a first-base coach chimes in. "Show him your mark."

The batter raises his sleeve to reveal a faint red place the size of an M&M. I approach the bench to contend the blemish could have gotten there any time in the ten years the kid has drawn breath.

The first-base coach insists the umpire look at the evidence. "If his arm is warm," he argues, "it must have just happened."

Determined not to let this guy out-Perry Mason me, I submit for the court's approval that the arm is warm because it has a shirt over it.

Mac offers another possibility. "Mark, schmark. The kid went to the clinic and got a shot."

The umpire refuses to check immunization records. We lose the judgment.

The unhit batsman is awarded first base.

Their clean-up hitter hits one over Walter's head in right and chugs to third before we can return the ball to the infield. The next pitch bounces off Evan's shin guards. Tie game. On to the eighth.

The Cubs give thought to plating the go-ahead run in our half of the inning, but decide it would be best to play on and keep the home-plate umpire from drinking beer with his friends.

Their guys don't have any say in the matter, going down one-two-three without hitting one past the pitcher's mound. On to the ninth.

It's getting dark. This will be the last inning. Coaches agree on sudden-death rules. No warm-ups. No infield ball. No outfield ball. Child-herder in on-deck circle to hasten arrival of batter to plate. If a kid can't find his glove, one will be provided for him. If a kid can't find his hat, who cares?

K. B. and Evan strike out. Danny walks.

I can barely see him. If I'm going to trace his path around the bases, Mac needs to give him a glowlight.

Adam pops up to short. The umpire says their kid caught it. I'll have to take his word for it.

Because I am cold and unfeeling, I bring in both my hardest and wildest pitcher to keep the opposition from taking back the night.

Vaughn.

Because Mac long ago learned to make do with materials at hand, he wraps a circle of adhesive tape on Evan's mitt. For good measure, he leaves a few strands on Evan's wrist. "I know you can't see, so throw to the white," he hollers to his son. A new catchphrase is born.

Their players are scared anyway. Now add a big kid of a pitcher attempting to hit a color-coordinated location without benefit of radar. Vaughn strikes out the side.

Tie.

His performance isn't quite worthy of a game ball, but Vaughn's welcome to all the adhesive tape he can scrape off Evan's glove.

Parents and players quickly disperse. I throw the bases in the shed and come back for the equipment.

Mac is waiting with a six-pack. "We ain't going nowhere."

I look at my watch for the first time since coming to the field. Allowing for the rain delay, we've been here more than three hours.

Seems like no time. "There is no place in the world I'd rather be than here," I say. "I wish we had forty more games."

We watch the outlines of a big kid and a little kid sliding into a water bottle of a second base.

"You squished it, tubby," Evan hollers.

Vaughn chases him into the black hole of the outfield.

"It's gonna kill us when we don't have kids to do this with any more," Mac says.

Silence.

That scenario too horrible to dwell on, we return to the precious present and plot strategy for the tournament.

"What are we going to do about Caleb?" I ask. "He's gone from being our best hitter to almost being another Walter."

"We bunt him," Mac says. "You remember the other night at the batting net when Graham was getting eaten up by chiggers and you went inside to get some lotion? "Caleb climbed in and I told him to forget hitting for a few minutes and concentrate on laying the ball down. You know he's the best athlete on the team. Well, he had ten straight perfect bunts before he popped one foul. When he squares around, it's like he thinks he has the bat to protect him and he's not scared."

"Good thinking. Now what about Evan not hitting when it means something?"

"Simple. Put blinders on him so he won't know we have baserunners."

Graham had a good day at the plate. They made a couple of good plays on him, but he hit four balls hard. I tell Mac about the little film session at his dad's house.

"Must've worked. You know that baseball card of his dad he always kept in his uniform pocket? Well, I always check the kids to make sure they're not packing anything that can cut their butts in case they have to slide. I had Graham empty his pocket and the only thing back there was a pack of Jolly Ranchers. How much do you think that weighs?"

"From four to six ounces, I guess."

"That baseball card of his dad had to come in at at least a ton. I'd say that's a good exchange."

"Ken's got to quit wearing that stupid suit to our games," I say.

"Make him work the concession stand," Mac suggests. "They say the popcorn popper almost exploded today. Nothing like the threat of second-degree burns to put somebody in T-shirt and jeans."

I tell him about Danny's decision not to go on vacation with his parents, and how I caved on the batting second thing.

Mac can't believe it. "Man, passing up Hawaii is big-time. Letting him keep his spot in the order wasn't enough. You should have given him controlling interest in the team."

I share one last piece of news. "Did you know that Walter is off probation?"

"How'd that happen?"

"His mother made him a proposition. Answer one question right and everything is square."

"What was it?"

"Name the largest city in New York State. Kid didn't even hesitate."

One kid forgets batting glove. One kid forgets wrist bands. One kid forgets Hooters poster.

17

THE PINCH-RUNNER STEALS THE SHOW

Today, Danny and his cell phone have company while waiting for the coaching staff and finding out about homework assignments.

Trent.

They throw while I talk with his dad.

"We can't keep him out of the hospital. He does real good for a few weeks and we put him back in school. Then the breathing problems come back and the doctors have to admit him to run more tests."

"His color looks better than it did two months ago," I offer.

"Maybe a little, but the bad thing is that he's down to forty-seven pounds. The weight just won't stay on."

I notice that he's in uniform.

"We thought maybe he could sit on the bench and be with the other boys."

I ask if he wants to play.

"God, yes. He's begged me, but the doctors would kill me. He's supposed to rest."

"Any good news on a cure for CF?"

"Just talk and some new somethings or others that they keep injecting him with that never do any good."

Again, I don't know what to say. Taking the team to Two-Bit Sports, I can do. Talking to the father of a sick child, I can't.

Caleb and I have a talk.

Me: "This is the play-offs. We need all of you out there today."

Him, disappointed in self: "I'm hitting like shit."

The rule on cussing is temporarily suspended.

Me: "Then pitch."

First inning.

Their lead-off batter hits a liner over Graham's head at shortstop. He goes to second on the next pitch when our catcher fails to block a pitch in the dirt. To make it look even more like he's just temporary help back there, he bounces the return throw to Caleb.

"Evan!" I hiss.

Seeing such slovenly play behind the plate, their coach figures third is a safe bet. So he sends his runner.

I don't blame him. We've botched this play all year. On those instances when Evan gets off a good throw, we either don't catch the ball or we don't execute the tag. Often it doesn't even get that far. Instead of coming up throwing, Evan comes up thinking.

The result? Bob Dole could steal third against the Plaza Cubs. But wait.

Evan comes out of his crouch and releases the ball more or less in one motion. No wasting of valuable time to make windage check. The throw is low. Even better than that, it's on the right side of third base.

Aaron straddles the bag. Aaron catches the ball.

But will he remember that the tag must be applied at ground level since the runner will be taking the low road?

Yes!

The umpire makes the only decision he can make when one boy is triumphantly holding the ball and the other boy is coughing up dirt that would have been carted away before the game had the dad assigned to that job not been called to try to put the popcorn popper back together.

"That," Mac declares, "was huge."

Indeed. It serves to assure Caleb that he's actually got some help out there.

Second inning. Danny jumps at least two inches to catch a line drive.

Still in second inning. One out. Man on second. Grounder to K. B. at third. He catches it over the bag and prepares to make the long throw to first, an iffy play at best at this level.

But wait.

The baserunner takes off for third. K. B. puts the ball in his glove and meets him halfway. The kid tries to go around him. K. B. tags him out. Great play.

Third inning. The throw from Graham short-hops Vaughn at first, but he scoops it. Another top-notch play.

Fourth inning. The Cubs administer a dose of the yeps. It starts with Danny, who goes "Yep, yep, yep, yep," in the manner of a small, obnoxious dog. Then a yep-yepping solo from Vaughn that sounds like "Happy Birthday." Then individual yeps until the entire ball diamond sounds like an out-of-tune metronome.

Not only are we talking a good game, we're hitting. Adam, Graham, Aaron, Felix, and, in a manner of speaking, Caleb.

Home half of the first. Two on. Two outs. Caleb lays a perfect bunt down the third-base line. Graham scores from second when their kid tries to get Caleb at first.

Home half of the third. Vaughn at third. Caleb bunts again,

this time to first. Their kid commits every fielding blunder imaginable save for digesting the ball. Cubs score.

Home half of the fourth. Their coach positions his infielders in an arc on either side of the pitcher's mound. One of his kids might get a baseball facial, but, by God, Caleb won't get another bunt down.

"They're waiting for you," I holler. "Gotta hit away."

He looks at me as if to say, hey, they can't play up like this, it isn't fair. Then he reverts back to the kid who has taken stepping in the bucket to a new level. It almost hurts to watch. A boy who is absolutely petrified.

Two strikes.

The coach moves his infielders back. No more dawn patrol.

Caleb squares around and cues the ball equidistant between the pitcher and first baseman. The real Cubs couldn't have thrown him out.

We go up thirteen to four.

Mac puts it in better perspective. "One team's gonna get eliminated today, and it ain't us."

Fifth inning. Evan leads off with a grounder that hits the third baseman's foot.

Trent's dad comes to the back of the dugout to give him some gum.

I get an idea.

"Can he run?"

"He's played around some in the yard, but that's about it," Trent's dad says. "Why?"

"I'll take Evan out and put Trent in. Pinch-runner."

Trent overhears, and starts tugging on his father's arm.

"You can't, son. Remember what the doctor said about throwing up if you exert yourself?"

"I've puked before, haven't I? It won't kill me. I'm gonna

run." Without waiting for a response, he puts on a helmet and takes off for first.

His dad doesn't try to stop him. "Looks like it's going to be a two-breathing-treatment night."

"Three," I say. "One for me."

The Cubs call time.

I have a meeting with Danny, Adam, and Vaughn—our next three hitters. My message is brief and to the point. "That little boy might be on base for the last time in his life. I want him to come around and score. You do whatever it takes to make that happen."

Wild pitch. Trent makes it to second, but he's really huffing and puffing. He bends over for a few seconds and then says he's OK.

Danny lifts a pop-up in back of the pitcher's mound that falls between three players. Trent doesn't know what to do so he stays put. Good decision.

The pitcher quickly gets two strikes on Adam. Trent hollers at him to get a hit. Adam steps out, and puts on a look I've seen before. When he gets back in, he stands maybe two inches from the plate. He leans over until almost half of him is in the strike zone. The next pitch is high. Adam doesn't move. The ball hits him in the shoulder.

Trent has completed three-fourths of his journey.

It takes Vaughn one pitch to make me cry.

Line drive to right. Trent can walk home. No panting. No hurling.

What happens next is just this side of a ticker-tape parade.

Trent's dad runs onto the field.

Trent's mom runs onto the field.

Mac runs down from first, grabs Trent, and hugs him.

The opposing coach, who knows the family, shakes Trent's hand.

The brick mason of a home-plate umpire, who doesn't know anybody but knows a moment when he sees one, gives Trent the ball.

Naturally, Caleb shuts them down in the sixth. Game over.

I give the shortest of post-game speeches. "Everybody did good."

Krishna rushes up to make an important announcement. He's rented the back room at a pizza place for a slide show that will tell the story of the season. Coaches and players are invited to watch as our innermost baseball moments are made public record.

Associated Press photographers during wartime have nothing on Krishna.

The man was in the dugout, in the batting net, in the on-deck circle, at the scorer's bench, even in the concession stand.

I had my back to the infield showing Felix how to stretch for a ball at first. Caleb threw a ball that caught me behind the ear. Krishna was there.

Danny answered his phone during a game. His mother wanted to remind him to feed the dog when he got home. Krishna was there.

Today's the day we find out if we were in focus.

"Come in, come in, everybody come in," Krishna says, directing us to our tables. A camera is around his neck. The good photographer never assumes pizza will be eaten without incident.

The first slide is of Mac's rear end. Nothing but.

"He's farting," Evan insists. "I can tell."

Krishna waits until the laughter dies down. Clearly, he has prepared this slide presentation to have the pacing and gamut of emotions you'd expect from a Broadway play.

"Here we have a close-up of Walter's face when he got hit during the first practice."

Then, "I did the exact same shot four weeks later. Notice the pattern of healing."

There's one of Evan looking for the ball after he's made a bad throw.

There's one of Vaughn taking a nap on his batbag.

There's one of an intense Krishna, taken by his wife, practicing his hitting at Two-Bit Sports. It will never be used in their advertising. The man looks like a crazed guerrilla leader plotting to overthrow the provisional government with a large stick.

The room is buzzing. The MC has to settle us down.

"Now if everybody will pay attention, here's a shot of Garret catching Caleb's fastball with his bare hands."

Aaron asks if it hurt. I tell him he won't see a slide showing the pattern of healing.

Back to Krishna. "This next shot is of Mac giving K. B. a high-five."

None of us are visually impaired, but Krishna insists on full IDs and full explanations. Understandable, I suppose, considering this is opening night.

"The last one in this sequence is of Garret after Danny hit one to the outfield. If you look closely, you can see the body English."

There's one of Aaron after he's thrown his glove.

There's one of flu-ridden Graham wiping snot off his nose.

There's a before-and-after shot of the face mask that shows how Mac fixed it.

"The next few," Krishna goes on, "are from a practice at the batting net." This picture is a steep decline from the artistry evident in the other slides. It's blurry and begs the question of why the photographer would aim at the hay bales in the first place.

"I remember that one," Mac chimes in. "Krishna wanted an action shot of a kid batting, so he rested the camera on the net.

Felix socked one about three inches from the lens. I thought Krishna was gonna shit, oops, go in his pants."

Krishna neither confirms nor denies and quickly goes to the next slide, which is of Evan showing the camera exactly how he throws his split-finger.

There's one of a seamer on Adam's arm.

There's a shot of K. B. trying to read the Braille message Chase sent me wishing the Cubs luck in the tournament.

"I close the show," the projection-meister says majestically, "with a special look at Vaughn's hotter."

"Heater," hollers everybody in the room.

The picture was taken an instant after the kid pitcher released the ball. There's no fooling the camera. Both eyes are closed.

In the next shot, Vaughn is eating a hotdog. His eyes couldn't be more open.

Big-time laughter.

"Hey, the boy knows how to set his priorities," Mac says.

18
AND GROWN PEOPLE WONDER

Hottest day of the year. At least ninety-five degrees by game time.

Moms pass out oranges and sports drinks. Dads encase heads in cold towels. Brothers and sisters put ice cubes inside caps.

"This is better than room service," K. B. says.

Trent's dad sticks his head in the dugout. "We were afraid Trent would get overheated, so we left him home. He wants a full report, though."

I ask Evan if he wants to split the catching duties with Graham.

He shakes his head.

This is partly because he is proud to be our primary catcher. It's also so he can tell everybody after the game that he was by far the most uncomfortable person on the field.

First inning. Grounder to Danny at second. He boots it. Then a one-hopper up the middle that Graham fields in back of the pitching rubber. He throws low and wide to Caleb covering second. No forceout. Pop fly to Vaughn at first, which he catches. Their lead runner is halfway to third before turning back. Vaughn fires to Caleb at second, but the throw is way high. The ball bounces into the culvert that was put in so something else could stink besides the outdoor toilet. They go on to score four runs.

Second inning. Evan throws a swinging bunt into right field. Aaron misses a fly ball in left. Caleb screws up a ground ball.

Third inning. Adam and Vaughn open with walks. Wild pitch. Adam moves to third, but Vaughn doesn't take a step off first. Aaron hits a sharp grounder up the middle. For some reason, their shortstop is playing almost beside second base. He catches the ball on the second hop, steps on the bag, and throws to first. Double play. We end up scoring a pair, but Vaughn's baserunning gaffe cost us an important out.

We're down eight to three. The game is delayed for a few minutes so the kids can cool off.

Mac whispers in my ear. "Money Ball." He goes to the concession stand to get some cups.

Time for a team meeting.

I ask Danny if he's hot.

"Boiling."

I ask if he's hotter than the boys in the other dugout.

"Yes."

Just the answer I wanted to hear.

"Why, Danny?"

"Because we've been out in the sun longer."

"Exactly. Do the fourth-graders on the other side of the field have stronger constitutions than you guys?"

"No."

"So, Danny, what would you say is the key to the Cubs mounting a comeback?"

"Make them stay out there until they start tasting their salt the way we're tasting our salt."

"Precisely. They're no better than we are," I go on. "We hit the ball and force them to make some plays, and I guarantee they'll start kicking it all over the lot."

I have the boys put their hands together and tell Aaron to lead us out.

"Let's fire up, guys," he says. "We don't want to do all this sweating for nothing."

Knute Rockne couldn't have given a better speech.

Mac is back with the cups. He rips open a ten dollar roll of quarters. "Time to increase your disposable income, men. Four quarters if you hit the ball and get on base. Six quarters if you hit the ball hard."

Fourth inning. K. B. dribbles one to third. Their kid comes up too late to make the play. Banker Krishna clinks his cup. Evan hits a dart to left field. More clinking. Adam singles to right. Vaughn sends one through the third-baseman's legs. Graham's fly ball goes in and out of the center fielder's glove. Aaron beats out a slow roller to second. Felix bounces one up the middle.

"Whoo, whoo," says Krishna as he tries to keep up with the payments.

Tie game.

But Felix can't hold them in the fifth. The first two kids get solid hits, and they move up on a wild pitch. The two-to-two pitch gets by Evan to the screen. Felix races up to cover home, but Evan throws the ball over his head. We're slow to react to the loose ball and the second runner scores.

Felix walks the next two batters, and I bring Aaron in. Good move. He gets three of the next four kids out, and they plate only one more run.

Fifth inning. Danny hits one the length of two batbags spread end to end. He looks down from first base to see Krishna holding up four fingers to match the number of quarters he awarded.

Their pitcher drops to his knees, a victim of the heat. A platoon of parents sprints to his aid, and the coach starts warming up his center fielder.

Our runner on first uses the time to argue that his hit was worth the full $1.50.

Danny: "It left the bat hard. I can't be responsible for what happens after that."

Krishna: "The ball could have hit your helmet and gone farther."

Danny: "If you consider I have a bad bat, it went pretty far."

Krishna: "No payment by the foot. This isn't the carpet store."

Mac checks his pockets in the first-base coaching box. Only three quarters left. "Make me go get some more," he hollers.

Opposing coach, grinning: "You realize this is a forfeit, don't you? Your players have lost their amateur status."

Adam sends Mac to the money store with a wicked grounder their third baseman wanted no part of. Vaughn follows with a hit and we're down one going into the last inning.

Aaron gets the first two guys easily.

Then we do something we haven't had to do all season.

Which is stand and watch a member of the opposing team circle the bases after ripping one over the fence.

The old Aaron would have thrown his glove and kicked the pitching rubber until it became unearthed. The new Aaron just turns red in the face, and has a meeting with himself in back of the mound.

We get out of the inning with no more damage. Cubs need two to tie.

"This is real simple, guys," I tell them. "Nobody makes an out."

Mac doesn't say anything. He just jiggles the money jar.

Caleb walks. Felix loops one to left, but their shortstop hauls it in with his back to the infield.

Walter ambles to the plate, but I call him to the third-base box. He expects a lecture, but I have another purpose. I put four quarters in his pocket. He looks at me funny. "Pre-payment," I explain.

He trickles one to the right side. The second baseman refers the grounder to the attention of the first baseman. The first baseman is completely unaware of his colleague's decision until after the play is over. In the confusion, Walter is aboard.

K. B. pops up. Two on. Two outs. Evan up. Crunch time. Pressure-packed moment. Joy of victory, agony of defeat.

So many cliches to pile on such little shoulders.

He taps the dirt off his size fours and prepares to stand in. Just enough time for a mini-debate.

Do I want him up there in this spot?

Certainly. He's one of our better hitters.

Absolutely not. Let some other father's son make the last out of the season.

I want to turn my back. If he does well, I'll hear it. If he doesn't, I'm a step closer to the outdoor toilet, where I'll remain for the rest of my natural life.

The first pitch is at his shoelaces. Doesn't matter. He swings. Strike one.

The next offering is equally flawed. At least a foot high. Again, it doesn't matter. Whiff.

Way outside. He swings. Foul ball.

Way inside. Swing. Another foul.

This is killing me. I don't mind moving to the toilet, but let's get it over with so I can go pick up my things.

Way low. Swing. Foul.

It's obvious that Evan is going to offer at anything that's pitched. All their kid has to do is fire one into the top of the screen and the game is over.

But wait.

The boy throws a strike.

Evan strides. Evan turns his shoulders. Evan rolls his wrists.

And hits the mother of line drives up the middle.

The pitcher, a quick thinker, has the following conversation with himself: Hmm, what could I do to ruin a glorious moment for the Cubs' organization? Answer: I know just the thing. Put my glove over my face in self-protection, and let the ball come in as per a stroke of dumb luck.

Which is what happens.

We lose.

Krishna drops the money jar.

Mac stomps first base.

I throw my hands up.

So close.

The town's women and children didn't get saved, but I see no need to move my record collection to the outdoor toilet. Evan did all right.

Disgust covers our faces as we make the death march to home plate to extend limp hands for the Red Sox to pretend to shake.

The mood lasts only until the boys get back to the dugout.

"Free cash," Danny yells as he spots several dollars' worth of spilled quarters.

Danny's parents can afford to make a down payment on a cruise ship, and here's Danny diving in the dirt for the money it will take to send his uniform through the laundry an extra time.

The other boys join in. I start to referee, but it's too much fun watching Aaron put his quarters in with his protective cup to make sure nobody steals any.

We finally get the boys settled down, so we can start the postseason ceremonies.

Caleb gives Trent's dad a quarter to take home to his son.

I give Krishna a madras shirt I found in the trash at work.

Mac gives me a used Gregg Typing Manual.

Mac gives Krishna a baseball. And why not—we finished the season plus nine.

I give Mac the before-and-after photographs of the face mask.

Time to say good-bye.

Mac first.

"I'm not much on speeches. I just want to say that I had a lot of fun, and I'm proud of every one of you little guys. You parents have a great bunch of kids, and you kids have a great bunch of parents."

That's being serious long enough.

"And now if you'll excuse me, I'm going to do a cannonball into the culvert."

Everybody laughs.

My turn.

"I'm going to try to get through this without crying. I'm never more alive than when I'm playing ball with a group of kids. I look forward to the season more than someone my age is supposed to, and every year it gets harder to say good-bye. I want you boys to know that I love each of you as a person. I wish we didn't have to get older. I wish we could keep it right here."

That's being serious long enough.

"Hey, Mac, get over here. I can strike you out."

We adjourn to the field. Kids are outfielders and ball-chasers.

Ken takes off his suit jacket and plays third base. Walter's mom borrows the catcher's mitt and plays deep left field foul territory. Krishna gets in the on-deck circle.

K. B. thanks me for not telling his parents about the Hooters poster.

Graham thanks me for helping him play better. He says the chigger bites are getting better every day.

Walter asks if I will be his coach again.

Mac steps up to the plate wearing a giant diaper.

And people wonder why a grown man would want to do this.